The Absence of Love

E-mail the author at spiritmeat@yahoo.com

The Absence of Love
A Story of Love Revealed

Sandra Lindsay

The Absence of Love: A Story of Love Revealed

©2012 by Sandra Lindsay

All rights reserved. No part of this book may be reproduced in any form without written permission from the author.

ISBN 978-1-300-41759-0

Lindsay, Sandra
The Absence of Love: A Story of Love Revealed

E-mail: spiritmeat@yahoo.com
Website: http://www.spiritualmeat.com

Edited by Stephen J. Porvaznik

Dust jacket photo credits:

  Front cover: Christine Martin
  Inside front: Kelly Kasey Photography (http://www.kellykasey.com)

Printed in the United States of America

Dedicated to Aunt Jo, my mother's best friend

Acknowledgements

I'd like to thank my husband Michael for his patience, support, and encouragement during the writing and editing of this manuscript–and for keeping me grounded. Thank you for being the earthly groom that this bride has needed.

Thank you also to Troy, Todd, Christy, and Christopher–for helping me discover what love means from a parent's perspective–and a child's.

Finally, thanks to my editor, Steve Porvaznik, for his guidance and expertise with the written word, helping me to clarify and expand on the truths in this book.

The Absence of Love

Prologue

The bride stood at the threshold, just around the corner from the aisle. The time had finally come. The preparations had been long, the wait seemingly endless. The proposal was made a long time ago, and the long engagement period had bonded them and brought them to this culminating event. Now, she was to be joined to her groom–the one whom she had been waiting for her whole life.

But, in the deep recesses of her mind, stuffed down just for awhile, was a past that she would one day need to assess. She would go through many struggles during this marriage–every relationship did. She wasn't thinking about any of that consciously on this day, of course. Still, it was there, and it began slowly rising to the surface.

She stared down at her right hand at the beautiful engagement ring he had given her long ago. It shone brightly, even in the dim room she was in, catching whatever light it could, reflecting it back. She turned her hand slightly back and forth, admiring it. Then, she felt a little sad. She wished she felt worthy of this gift he had given her, this commitment he made to her.

During the engagement, she had many questions, many doubts. It was a love story, for sure, but one which shared what all stories share–conflict. She questioned her readiness, her worthiness, of this man she was getting to know, who would soon be taking her as his bride. She knew now that she loved him, and desired more than anything to spend the rest of her life with him.

She had decided to make that commitment, to say "Yes", to put her faith and trust in him. She realized he loved her with the kind of selfless, sacrificial love that only a true soul mate felt for his partner. More than that, she realized that he had loved her long before she fell in love with him.

He loved her in a way that no one ever had before, and ever would again. She was more precious to him than the most valuable jewel that could ever be dug out of the deepest mine. He accepted her flaws, her past, her mistakes–everything that she could throw at him, and all the baggage she brought with her. He was unrelenting in his love and acceptance of her. No matter what situation she faced, he was there to comfort her. Her friends called him Mr. Perfect, and it was true–he was without blemish, without stain. She longed to be like him in that way.

Yet, wasn't he a man like other men? She had known many others, had even committed her life to others in the past (or so she thought), but they failed to live up to the wants and needs she had in a marriage partner. But, no, he was not like all the others. He was different. He was the one!

~

For those who are married or who have been there, you can appreciate the feelings this bride is going through. When we finally meet that "one" to share our life with, there is almost nothing that compares to that sense of contentment and peace that a life-long partner brings. Still, we are only human, and therefore, far from perfect. We are flawed, and so will be our human relationships, try as we might to keep them together and cycle through the mistakes, pain, suffering, forgiveness, and reconciliation that have to occur over and over again to maintain those relationships.

But, I want to tell you about a different kind of relationship, the kind that brings more fulfillment and ultimately provides that lasting comfort and eternal peace that other earthly relationships do not. It is the greatest love story ever told–an historical romance of our God and His intense love of His creation, humankind. That includes you and me!

Consider for a moment those things in your life which have become precious. What makes something "precious", so valuable that it separates itself from everything else? Why is that something so precious, so valuable, so worthy of holding up in such high regard? Was it a price you paid for that thing? Was it a monetary price, or was it a sacrifice that had to be made to get it?

I would like to suggest to even the most materialistic of this world that those things most precious to us have been purchased with a price. Yet, real value is found in the cost of the labor required to earn said payment.

Even the steepest payment cannot match that of the eternal Creator's. While we were still flawed human beings (the Bible calls that "sinners"), God so loved us that He sent His only son, Jesus Christ, to labor on our behalf, to rekindle, renew, and revive a separated people to the original Creator. The price? His life blood! Imagine sacrificing your own son! Anyone with children would agree that they are the most precious thing in the world, and offering them up to be tortured and killed would be the most supreme sacrifice that anyone could make. And Jesus, who was both fully man and fully God, took on this pain and suffering willingly, and, by doing so, took on our sins. Then, when He died and came back to life, He became the way for all of us to experience eternal life with Him.

As human beings, we are like a diamond in the rough to God. Yes, indeed, beauty in the eyes of the beholder can turn a hunk of coal into a shining jewel. Turning each one of us into this jewel is a gift from God who loves us unconditionally.

This, then, is a story of the One who loved His people deeply. His love was dedicated to the eternal well-being of each one of us. Each of us is a life created by His Spirit–birthed, kept, and matured during our lifetime on Earth and on into the next life.

The truths presented in this book will manifest God's ultimate purpose: to prepare a bride without spot or blemish for an eternal life together with Him. In fact, this love story is the betrothal of the Bride–Christ's Church–to the groom–Jesus Himself, our redeemer and God's sacrifice and gift to us.

How this is accomplished is the plan by which Christ died and was resurrected, making salvation available to all. The Bible, God's word, is the "guide" revealed for this preparation. Like a plant that brings forth good fruit, this guide explains how love is nurtured and, through the work of that Spirit, we can develop the fruits of those labors, share in the gifts, and experience that ultimate expression of love available to all of us in Christ Jesus.

Love, then, is the motivation that can turn that "absence"–the emptiness and loneliness we experience as humans–into the full "presence" of God, joined ultimately as His bride at the wedding feast.

Chapter One
Love Covenant

Her dress was a shimmering spectacle–white, beaded, flowing. She seemed to radiate her own light, as a full moon is lit up by the sun. Her luminance brightened the shaded waiting room she was standing in. She knew, though, that it was all appearance. She was a fireball of emotions inside, trying to hold it all together. She was about to experience something that all girls dream their whole lives of experiencing. It was to be the most important, most memorable day she would ever have up to this point–to be joined for eternity with the one who would make her life complete. Yet, she felt undeserving of his love. No, she *was* undeserving of his love!

Indeed, she felt incomplete without him. She had been lonely for a long time, even during the years when she was in other relationships and had many friends and acquaintances to call on for counsel and help her through the rough times. But, until she met him, she didn't realize the enormous hole she had in her life that was never to be filled by anyone or anything else–not the well-meaning people in the clubs, organizations, and churches she joined, nor the many indiscretions she indulged in when she was at her lowest point.

Fortunately, her veil had been lowered for quite a while

now, as she waited for her time to walk down the aisle. It obscured her face. In her mind, she simply focused on him, and that brought great comfort to her. She felt overwhelmed, but she knew, with him standing by her side, she would be able to grow into the person she was meant to be. He promised her that, and she knew he would keep that promise. He was committed to her, and had been for quite awhile. It was she that took time to truly commit to him, but when she did, she experienced a peace in her soul that she had never experienced before. What he didn't promise was that her life would be easy.

~

What kind of love story would it be without a commitment? A commitment is required for a relationship to endure. Many have tried to engage love without that commitment, without dedication, without the endurance required. The result is not so different from those who engage in relationships in which a vow is made out of our own selfish desires–our "sinful nature"–without the knowledge of "true love". Relationships then, either exist without love or out of convenience, or both. Let me suggest that this "true love" I am talking about is the one written about long before my knowledge of it came into existence. Unfortunately we may well be more familiar in this world with the love deployed by our sinful nature.

Therefore, to continue my journey on these pages, you will need to begin to dream. You know that dream some little girl or boy had when they thought about "life", and what it could really be for them. Do you remember?

A Little about Me

I am a dreamer. As a child growing up in a small town in the Midwest, there was plenty of time to daydream. We could run and play in much of the town because everyone knew who we belonged to. Our yard was big enough to have softball games and most of the neighborhood kids showed up on a regular basis.

Our family was well known in Cornell, Illinois, a country town of five hundred people. We attended the First United Methodist Church. All the other denominations were represented in this town as well. My father was well-respected at church. He taught the youth and often was given responsibility that put him in the pulpit to speak on Sunday mornings. Mom would always prompt him when speaking to take the keys out of his pocket so he wouldn't rattle them while he spoke. From the time I was born through elementary school (eighth grade), we were in church when the doors were open.

My sister Sharon was three years older than me. My brother Larry was thirteen months younger. After Larry was born, sis became more of a mother to me. Mom was busy caring for our newborn brother. Because money was scarce in our family, Mom sewed most everything we wore–from winter coats to prom dresses. That takes time, so, by the time I was ten years old, my sister and I were cooking regularly for supper and doing the dishes. Sis and I were also required to clean house on Saturdays. That always annoyed me because other children my age were outside playing on that day.

Our mother never seemed pleased about her station in life. I seemed to hold the focus of her disappointment. Pleasing her was never really an option for me. Whatever I did seemed to irritate her. I believe I challenged her in just about every area of living from a very young age. This did not fare well for me in life. I was said to be a ball of fire and hard to control by the time I was three years old. I was alive!

Sometimes dreams are created to imagine how life could be different. I wanted to be loved. I wanted to feel good about myself. I wanted my life to matter. And I wanted to be validated. I seemed to be able to do this at school and in extracurricular activities. Where my life was not acceptable was at home.

Our father worked endless hours. He was a mechanic. Dad started his own business and this kept him away from home a lot of hours. Sometimes, he would work more than one job to make ends meet. Dad always provided for our family's needs, but the trade off was his absence a great deal of the time from our lives. Still, he was my soft spot. When times were difficult, I knew Dad loved me. This became a rift in my life too. I don't know if Mom was jealous of my relationship with Dad or what. I do remember she used to say, "If you want something from Dad, ask Sandy to get it from him."

I was excited about living. The endless possibilities of what I might do were thrilling to me. Why, it was the "All American Dream"! What I didn't realize was that that takes money, which always meant more responsibility for my parents.

I dreamed and hoped for an adventurous life. To make this happen, my focus early on involved trying to find love, which, inevitably, led to bad choices and wrong decisions.

What About You?

How much was love a part of your formative years? Were you nurtured? Cared for? Truly loved? If not, or not as much as you should have, this book and the story it shares may be extra hard to take on board in your life. If, however, you desire to know what is missing in your life, you may be able to find yourself and what is lost or simply misplaced somewhere in these pages. Maybe you can hope again, with a hope that will not disappoint you.

Those who know this story will already know the kind of hope that does not disappoint. It can be difficult to find in this world. The absence of it, at any point in time, does not mean it did not exist. It means only that we–you and me–decided to make our own way. No matter how knowledgeable or unschooled you may be, love can find a way into your heart, enabling hope to blossom again. Listen! I hear wisdom making its way into your future. Love is everything you ever dreamed it would be.

In The Beginning

The first mention of love from our guide, the Bible, is

found in Genesis, the first book. In the beginning! Imagine that? From the very beginning, love was involved in our creation. I have often heard the opposite from people whom I've loved and certainly a plethora of others whom I did not. What my grandfather said to me after living most of his life was, "If there is a God, why does He allow so much suffering"? Sound familiar to anyone else? I loved my Grandpa!

Grandpa showed he cared for me with his kindness and his sense of humor. He'd tell stories that Grandma didn't want repeated and we would laugh. He and Grandma had a farm in the heart of Illinois, the heartland of the United States. I never saw either of them in church for anything but a wedding or funeral. Still I knew, they loved me. How? Why? And how did this love leave, especially Grandpa, so jaded?

I shouldn't get ahead of my story, so the answers to those questions will have to wait. Perhaps in this book some of those questions will be answered. Hopefully, some of your questions about love will be too.

So on with the first mention of love from our guide in Genesis from creation. Yes, creation. Not evolution, not the big bang, but creation. You know the story or have some memory of reading or hearing your version of the beginning–don't you? Well, our story of love happens at the dawn of creation according to our guide. I think it is the birth place of love, according to many other resources as well. Why true love escapes us in our lives is a wonder, isn't it? From the Creator's point of view, I believe the feeling, as they say, is mutual. How could we miss it?

Exactly what took place in the creation of love for us? The story is old and it can often seem fragmented. Still, love has endured. In the beginning, I submit to you that "love" itself created the heavens and the earth, as well as its plan for the created–you and me.

When a newborn child comes into this world today, we often hear comments that there was no user's guide that came with their entrance into our lives, as if they were a refrigerator or a stereo that had an owner's manual or instructions at the time of purchase. But, we actually *do* have this owner's manual, this user's guide! It's called the Bible. We'll continue to reference this "guide" throughout this book to emphasize or explain certain points we're making.

At the beginning of this journey, our adventure is to acknowledge that love not only created us, but planned for us a life of unimaginable fellowship with that Creator. As the tagline from the Steven Spielberg classic *Close Encounters of the Third Kind* says it, we are not alone! But, we're not talking alien beings here.

Love prefers light, though darkness exists. Love prepared room for us to live and have our being. Our guide calls it "expanse"–an area, span, spread, or vastness. At this point, there was no place for living things to breathe. However, this place was definitely in the plan. It seems this breathing was going to require air and dry ground, so love too created this. Now, apparently from the very beginning, we were going to need to eat! (Here's a big "Amen" to that from me.) The land produced vegetation: plants bearing seed according to their kind, and love said, "It is good"! Though darkness existed first, love further defines it with light (stars) in the expanse of the sky. Apparently, our eyes were never made to see without light and lots of it.

My daughter, Christy, is pleased that love did not yet stop creating. You see, she "loves" animals. She always has. I remember cleaning the bird seed around the cage where Christy's parakeet called home in her bedroom. When the morning sun filtered through the long narrow windows in her room, it was that little bird that lit up Christy's face. It was unconditional love in a world where love often came with a cost for her.

I think the foundation of Christy's fondness for animals is this: "Animals don't hurt you like people do". Now, you and I know they can hurt us, but somehow, even if that occurs, it is not as though they were mindful of such, even if we might become dinner to one of them! Anyway, love created animals and fish and birds and saw that it was good. I'm here to tell you my daughter Christy agrees.

Many years ago I asked myself, "What in the world did love see?" when creating all of this. I've had a good idea a time or two in my life, and have even developed and implemented some of these ideas, of which the results were not always all that good. How did love know everything it created was "good"? What about snakes? What about mosquitoes? How about great white sharks? Fungus? Cockroaches? I suppose many of my readers wonder that too.

Our guide tells us that our Creator, when creating each thing, "saw that it was good". A short study of the word "saw" will quickly paint a picture–a good metaphor, as it's something we need to see to appreciate. However, all of the senses, not just sight, are incorporated in the definition of "saw". Like creating beautiful art, God's act of creation was an emotional expression of love that touched all the senses. If you see, hear, taste, touch, or smell it, it will evoke emotion. When he "saw" that it was good, all of these senses were in operation. An individual who says love is without one or more of our five senses does not experience what was "seen" at creation by love.

Why did he create some things that we as humans view as "bad"–like the aforementioned mosquitoes–with no seemingly positive reason for existing? The short answer is that everything has a purpose, even if we as humans do not "see" it. (If we studied the biological, chemical, and ecological science behind some of these things, I believe we would see purpose for these things more clearly, but that's for a different book.) In short, love saw the purpose in each and every thing it created, so it was all "good" to Him.

Love also saw, as perhaps none of us could have, that to reproduce, seasons would be provided. It was true for plants and animals. It was also true for love's sixth thought. To add to his creation so far–light, the heavens, stars, vegetation, animals–what did God have in store that he would continue with his greatest creation yet? We could not have seen what love "saw". It's the one about creating a being in His image.

When love saw that *this* was good, there was enjoyment. There was great pleasure, in fact, in this new creation, love's greatest creation. A purpose was beheld, and there was human life!

And God saw everything that he had made, and, behold, it was very good. Genesis 1:31

After the sixth day, when he created human beings to have dominion over all other living things, it was especially good to God. The addition of the superlative "very" (in the Hebrew, the word for "very good" is *tov meod*) emphasizes the pleasure God received from this new creation, and He delighted in it.

However, some argue that this word also indicates that, for man, there is good and evil connected with it, because this word is also associated with extreme human pleasure. The word is one superlative below the Hebrew word for "very very good" or–even higher than that–"perfect", which excludes the "evil" connotation. For human beings, this kind of "seeing" we've been talking about evokes good and bad. It causes us to see with pleasure, as well as experience evil. God's creation was good, and the humans created were pronounced "very good". However, when sin entered the world, these human beings became flawed. All living things acquired the quality of decay and would eventually die. But, that was all part of love's plan too.

Covenant of Love

Our purpose for being created was clarified early on by our guide. It was spoken in covenant between Abraham, considered the father of the Jewish faith, and God (Genesis 15:18). In this covenant, there is an alliance as well as a pledge; a divine ordinance with signs, considered by the definition of covenant to be a messenger or declarer who is focused in on His creation. The purpose is two-fold and is declared in what is called a "covenant of love".

The first mention of the covenant of love is shared this way:

I am God Almighty; walk before me and be blameless. I will confirm my covenant between me and you: You will be the father of many nations. I will make you very fruitful. I will make nations of you and Kings will come from you. I will establish my covenant as an everlasting covenant between me and you and your descendants after you for the generations to come, to be your God and the God of your descendants after you. I will give an everlasting possession to you and your descendants after you; and I will be their God. Genesis 17:1-8

It is impossible to make a covenant with a person you do not know. Abraham knew God. God makes Himself perfectly known in this scripture. I am God. Regardless of your definition of God, this is a confirmation of the relationship Abraham was having with whom he had been in fellowship with. "I am God Almighty," He says.

What strikes me about God's acknowledgment of Himself was that Abraham knew Him. Like Noah, an established relationship with God was responsible for the response of each man. Who builds a ship in the middle of a desert? Noah! What rational man would do such a thing?

All of us wonder from time to time in our lives who God is. Our own heart condition can contribute to the answer, and I suggest to you that it did in both Noah and Abraham's lives. God made Himself known to both and the responses were decisions significant in each man.

Here's what the requirement was for both men to establish this kind of response in them.

Know therefore that the Lord thy God, he is God, the faithful God, which keepeth covenant and mercy with them that love him and keep his commandments to a thousand generations. Deu.7:9

Who Are You In Covenant With

When reading the scripture in Deuteronomy 7:9, what did you hear? Did you hear first it is important to "know"? This is another marvelous word that you should ahead of time realize has six and a half columns of information on it in the Bible concordance that I use. (For those that don't know, a concordance is a resource book for studying scripture.) There is an uncompromising assurance that can come when a human being, any human being, receives what God gives us to "know". I won't address this further, but I do suggest that each person settle this inside of themselves. God has no problem talking to us.

The character of the persons we might enter into agreement with should be established if in fact we expect any contract to be fulfilled. God's character is addressed in the above scripture. He says He is faithful. He assures us He keeps His promise. At the same time, God knows His creation and so He adds the idea of forgiveness to this initial covenant of love. He's teaching us while He is in fellowship with us!

God tells Abraham that His mercy for him is now engaged in the drawing up of this contract, but not just for him whom God loved, but for anyone who would love Him. The instruction that God continues to share in this "covenant of love" connects us to Him. We become partakers of this covenant when we agree to 1) love Him and 2) keep his commandments. In fact, the keeping of the commandments should be a result of that love for God.

If you love me, keep my commandments. John 14:13

Someone may be thinking, "I knew there was a catch." But, how can two be in covenant with each other and walk together unless they agree? God's commandments were written because He loves us.

We can banter about what love is, but at the end of the day my definition has become this: God is love! I will defer to yours if it is differently defined only if we abandon the story this kind of love, God's love, has written. In other words, it's another conversation for a different day. Today, anyone who can hear my voice: God is Love!

Keeping the Covenant

Love decides that once we make the decision to love God that we are to keep his commandments. Before I address "commandment", let us understand what "keep" means. Every contract, once it is complete, requires a set of skills to maintain it. There is a persistence required in the definition. We cannot carry on, or persevere. if a decision is not made to keep the agreement. You are the only party that is held responsible in your circumstances. It doesn't matter what the other guy does or doesn't do when we approach God about a matter. He will first and foremost address, "Did *you* decide to love Him? And then did *you* maintain *your* agreement with Him"?

Remember that God told Abraham to know the Lord is God and He is a faithful God. He *will* keep this love covenant even when we fail. He cannot be defeated when it comes to loving us. That's why we cannot please God without faith. He's saying that He can be trusted. He's saying that, even if we make a mistake, His love can make a way where there seems to be no way. He will not be defeated by darkness. He saw its presence in the midst of creation and declares it is okay. Nothing will separate us from the love of God! Once we make the commitment in our hearts that God is who He says He is, love has what it takes for this relationship to overcome every obstacle.

Like a groom asking a bride to marry him, God proposes to you and me early on in the story of our lives. He knows love. He *is* Love and it is everything you think love is and more! What will your answer be? And, what did you agree with God to do in addition to loving Him? In this dialogue, we are discussing the covenant of love we are to keep and the decision we made to love God. He not only built into this contract His knowledge of our imperfection to do so by incorporating His mercy and forgiveness, He also brings clarity to the table. He brings training into light. He educates us further by instructing us to keep His commandments.

Contingency Clause

Commandments are directives. Love originally gives us the instruction through the Ten Commandments. Anyone interested can find these written in Exodus 20:3-17. Because of sin in us, however, God had a contingency clause built into this love covenant. Let's address the covenant from this clause.

God knew His creation as well as he knew the darkness that came before it, and the darkness that would come after it. He knew the possibility that our freedom to choose to love Him would engage the "darkness" in our lives. Our circumstances can often lead us to responses that stem from our lack of training and inability to comply with God's covenant of love. God's love for us, built into this contract, enabled us to overcome our own insufficiencies as long as we were able to maintain our decision to love God.

He bound this agreement in blood, first with Abraham's blood, and then through the blood of Jesus. This confirmation is the contingency that love wrote into the document.

Whoever follows me shall not walk in darkness, but shall find the light of life. John 8:12

He overcomes the darkness in us each time we decide we will continue to love and follow Him. He made a way for us to keep His commandments, thereby honoring our choice to do so. Sheesh! How do we miss God's choice to love us even when our decisions do not properly respond to Him? How do we blame Him when we struggle to maintain our side of that covenant of love? What do we have in view when we decide so convincingly that it is God, and not us, who has fallen short on His faithfulness?

Me and Love

Having found the counterfeit of love many times before the reality set in, I should possibly be writing about what love is not. I had a great deal of life experiences qualifying me to expound further on my failures. This story will touch on some of that, but this book will not belabor these failures because of the resulting find in my life. It demands that the story be told about love, and about being truly "in love" with the "One True Love".

What happened to me? How can I now so easily write, "God is Love"? What took me from searching and searching earnestly for love and not finding it to this bold statement?

Let's continue the adventure of life in love. Let's marvel at His ability to show us a way we have never been before while realizing from the very beginning that Love finds a way.

Chapter Two
My Life and Love

Make every effort to add to your faith goodness; and to goodness, knowledge; and to knowledge, self-control; and to self-control, perseverance; and to perseverance, godliness; and to godliness, brotherly kindness; and to brotherly kindness, love. For if you possess these qualities in increasing measure, they will keep you from being ineffective and unproductive in your knowledge of our Lord Jesus Christ. II Peter1:5-8

The bride thought back to the first moment when she met her groom that long time ago. When she walked into that room at the party and first laid eyes on him, she was stunned by his presence. Even across the room, he was so handsome, even beautiful, though that word seems inappropriate to describe a man, but beautiful is what fit him.

    The room was crowded. Her date excused himself to go get drinks and meet up with a couple friends, and she was relieved. She wanted to find out who this new man was. He was speaking, and she stepped over a little closer to hear what he was saying. He was standing amongst several people, and they all wanted his attention, and were captivated by him. Somehow, he was able to give that attention to everyone who required it. He was a great listener, and only spoke when words were needed to be said, and it always seemed to be the right words, even if it wasn't what the person he was speaking to wanted to hear.

The Absence of Love

He was an amazing combination of opposites. He commanded attention, yet was humble and unassuming. Like those old E.F. Hutton commercials, when he talked, people listened. It was the way he spoke that was most peculiar, considering what he said seemed to come from someone with much authority and wisdom. He spoke with this gentle, kind voice. When he was standing close, you would almost call it a whisper.

Yet, although it seemed he always had something important to say, he didn't always say it–at least not with words. He was kind in a way that would make Mother Teresa proud. Even before the bride knew him, he traveled around the world in many humanitarian efforts. People at this party were asking him about some of these adventures, and he was reluctant to talk about what he had done. He only wanted to talk about what would come–his plans for the future. They pressed him for information, and he did relate some of the things that were witnessed by the people he visited. What the bride heard was unreal to her.

She never heard of someone doing the kinds of things he did, or the reason he did them. His selflessness had no bounds. He went into areas that many deemed unfit or unwise to venture, including dangerous terrorist areas. He spent time with people that were rejected by everyone else in that area–the derelicts and discarded of society. He was always ready to give of himself, to sacrifice, even if it meant giving up his own comfort and needs to meet the needs of others. He was persistent in lending that helping hand, even in the face of adversity. He pressed on deeper into areas and even to those who initially would not accept him. Even when the groups he led could not go with him anymore, he continued. He had his followers, but he also had many detractors–even enemies.

He had an extreme ability to maintain a peaceful demeanor, even when people disagreed vehemently with his views–and there were many dissenters ready to argue with him. There always are, when someone's message is to love *all* people, even those who despise you.

~

Summer Camp

It was 1963. I was thirteen years old and I was at summer camp for the second year at Epworth Springs, Illinois. The first year I attended was marked in my memory with my first–albeit quick–kiss. Was it possible I would receive another kiss this year? Instead, I had a different intimate encounter that would be another first for me.

Keith Sawyer, the boy that kiss was bestowed upon that first year, was not at camp for the second. Epworth Springs' cabins were constructed on rolling grass hills. There was a forested area bordering the hills. This summer, campers would work together to create a small camp fire with a cross behind it. We were instructed by our counselors to also erect an altar made from small trees from the underbrush. It was labor intensive–not conducive to the atmosphere of a second kiss I was hoping for.

Evening came and large numbers of children with their camp counselors made their way to our newly constructed outdoor version of the "upper room" like the one in the book of Acts that the disciples of Jesus stayed and had their devotions. I don't remember if there was a time of devotion brought to us by the adults who were supervising or not. What I do remember is bowing to my knees where that newly constructed "tree" altar was. Sally Sprague, our camp counselor, instructed the girls in our cabin to be silent and she knelt down next to me. The camp fire now illuminated the wooden cross, and I closed my eyes.

I don't know how long I was on my knees. I do know that I didn't get up until my counselor softly touched my hand. It was then I realized everyone else had returned to our designated area on the hillside.

Sally Sprague, a woman I knew only this one week of my life, gave all the girls pen and paper to write about our experiences that night. I didn't really understand the significance of the task she asked us to do that evening, nor what she would do with this information when we gave it to her.

Months later, I received a Christmas card with that hand written note enclosed. I recalled clearly the Lord's appearance to me. He appeared to me that night at the camp, but I was confused at first. Then, I realized I was hearing His voice. He asked me if I would follow Him that night. I wrote my answer on that piece of paper: "I know you are real, but I am not ready to follow you yet. I am looking for love!" I left Him hanging at the altar, so to speak. Fortunately, Love is patient.

Looking for Love

While seeking love myself in my early years, I was disheartened at home and in the world. The next year after that summer camp experience, I graduated from eighth grade. It was a prestigious moment. The awards validating me were unexpected. Though I considered myself a leader of my class, and had become a cheerleader in eighth grade, I had not expected to win a choir award with my voice.

The validation of graduation was short-lived. Our parents moved and the only world I had grown up in would no longer be a part of my life. A new adventure had begun.

The backdrop regarding our move included a great deal of tension between our parents. Mother did not want to move. My sister would live in Cornell to complete her last year of high school with our grandparents, while I would begin my first year at Streator High School. My brother, Larry, would make the move with us, but would remain in middle school, so I would make my way in high school alone.

Sports would not dominate my daily life as it had growing up. My new neighbor invited me to a party (girls only) where the key conversations were about boys! Little did I realize how competitive I had become. My first opportunity to find love would be a process that would discover something largely more qualified to be called lust. My new sport!

I didn't make the cheerleading squad in high school. I couldn't be in band and chorus, so I gave up singing. I managed to graduate from high school with a 3.2 GPA. Still, in that quest to find love, I came up empty.

Right out of high school, I entered Weaver Airline School. I wanted to broaden my horizons, and travel was the only desire I had apart from looking for love. American Airlines hired me and I moved to Chicago, Illinois. I was brought up in small town USA, so I was not very well-prepared for big city life. The adventure I had hoped for to find love was not what I found.

Two years went by while working for American Airlines. Though there were many adventures in travel, my search for love didn't turn up what I was looking for. My first roommate's family invited me for a visit. I remember them talking to me about God. My second roommate found love and got married. After several frightening experiences in Chicago where my life was threatened, I returned to my parent's home in Streator, Illinois.

Why would anyone return to a place they hadn't found love? I guess it was because it was still safe.

My eldest son Troy was born August 19, 1971. Now it was a fight for both of us to survive, but I had indeed found my first love! The marriage failed because once again I found myself in an environment that was not safe. Could life really be so difficult?

My motivation for my second marriage was desperation. I was desperate to find love, and have a life apart from my parents' home. The idea of being thankful could have possibly changed that, but my relationship at home had deteriorated.

Todd, my next son, was born on November 29, 1973. He was my second great love. My parents had made it clear that the life I was embarking on at 23 was not meeting with their approval. Moving back home this time was not a possibility. It never occurred to me that I could not make it on my own with two young sons to train up in the way they should go.

Condemning tones of my insignificance from those who I associated with, combined with my internal desire to find love, created a battle inside of me I just didn't understand. But, true love is persevering, invaluable, and powerful–so powerful that "nothing can separate us from the love of God" (Romans 8:38-39). It's a good thing, because I was on a path that would have most certainly led to my destruction and nearly did while I was continuing to look for love.

What I did find is that the qualities spoken about in the opening scripture were able to keep me from being "ineffective and unproductive" in finding love. This had nothing to do with my knowledge of them. It was the Holy Spirit's knowledge of them that I learned. I will describe this Spirit in more detail as this book progresses.

Adding Qualities to Your Faith

Here is the list of the qualities, contained in II Peter 1:5-7, that we are talking about that must be added to each other:

- Faith
- Goodness
- Knowledge
- Self control
- Perseverance
- Godliness
- Brotherly Kindness
- Love

According to this scripture, it is these qualities that, when added in increasing measure, keep us from being "ineffective and unproductive" in our knowledge of Jesus, our groom. This scripture indicates several things in this quest of this knowledge. One, that we need to "make every effort", which implies that it is a choice and that it will take work. Making this effort is not an easy task, but we must choose to do it and, when we do, it will be a progression–it will take time. It will not happen overnight, which is why the apostle Paul talks about making "every" effort. Many individual efforts, many days of work, many hours of toiling, will be required in this building of our knowledge of Jesus. That progression is also shown in the use of the order of the qualities–one leads to another.

It starts with faith as the foundation–all other qualities are added to our belief and underlying faith for our knowledge to grow. It continues with goodness, followed by knowledge, then self-control, then perseverance, and so on. One must be added on to another, ultimately leading to that fullness of love. Love, then, is the last quality that all others progress to in acquiring the "knowledge" that we need to be ready to be the Bride of Christ that we are destined to be when we truly "know" Jesus as our groom.

These qualities also have many overlapping themes to the "fruits of the Spirit" found in Galatians 5:22-23 which are described in chapters later in this book, so I won't go into them in detail here. Suffice it to say that these qualities ultimately come from the Holy Spirit, that third God-person of the trinity, that inner voice, the one that Paul, John, and other writers from the New Testament, as well as Jesus himself, speak of that help guide that inner knowledge and growth in us as Christians to help prepare us for the "wedding feast", another concept that is described in detail later.

Seeking Answers in the Church

It is with some sadness here that I must report that the Church, in its difficult task and the hard work required to be that primed-and-ready Bride, seemed helpless in my personal quest to find love and develop those sought-after qualities. The Church is made up of many individuals–humans who are flawed, try as we might to be that shining example of Jesus that we would like to be. Yet, I still expected my fellow believers to help me in my pursuit. But, the Church seemed unable to see my pain. And when it did, why didn't it help me? I was certainly there–at the church building, at least–and even attending one regularly most of my developing years.

I'm sure I presented a challenge even to the Church. Whatever I did, I always did it with all my might. If this kind of energy is properly directed, it can be a real asset. Mine was not.

I Couldn't Give What I Didn't Have

One thing I had learned in life is that you cannot give love if you do not have it. What did that say about my home and, worse yet, about the Church?

What it does say is that, in my quest to find "true love", the false, counterfeit, deceptive variety of love was far more indulging in my world. It treated me as if "the absence of love" was the fulfillment of my mission, but the battle to find love that had begun in me years ago continued to rage. What I found was ultimately empty and unfulfilling, and I could not settle for it. Somehow I knew that Love (the one with a capital "L") would not fail, but my attempts to locate it did.

Is it possible to legislate morality? It was immorality that found its way into my heart while I was looking for love. What could have stopped that? Looking for love in all the wrong places opened my heart up to one disappointment after another. I hadn't found love, but I had found a plethora of other parts of my own sinful nature.

It is unimportant for me to dialogue with you about all of my failures. It is enough to tell you they were all significant and costly to many people besides me. I really was without excuse because God is more than able to do all things, yet I was the one who told Him, "not yet"!

At a Crossroad

Finally, two marriages, two children, and two divorces later–all by the time I was 25 years old–I found myself at a crossroad. I had no more ideas and very little will left to go on. In pure desperation, I said to God, "If there is anything you can do with anything that is left of me, you can have me."

I didn't deserve a thing in that place I was calling out from, but somehow God calculated my worth differently. I hadn't decided to live differently, but my heart was now more compliant. I didn't know the way–what a revelation to admit to!

God's great gift to me was that while I was yet a sinner, He decided to die for me. For God so loved the world that He gave his only son for me, that whosoever (I was a whosoever) believeth in Him would not perish (John 3:16). What a life it was for me, but what a life I still had to live!

Chapter Three
Life by the Spirit

So I say, live by the Spirit. Galatians: 5:16

The time was fast approaching for her to walk down the aisle, but she still had a few moments to reflect on her past leading up to this point. When she first met her groom at that party, she was struck by his presence. Although she later realized it was a love-at-first-sight experience for him, it wasn't for her. She wasn't ready to fall in love yet–at least not with someone like him. She realized that a life with him would not be easy. He set the bar very high, and she knew it was difficult to live up to that standard. In fact, she thought it would be easier to continue on with the life she had been living. She did that for awhile.

She met many people and experimented with all kinds of lifestyles and activities, many she wasn't proud of and too embarrassed to admit, even to her closest friends or professional counselors she consulted with. She became obsessed with pleasure, and sought it in many ways. Yet, she soon realized that something was missing in her life, and she was desperately trying to fill it with anything that would hold off that empty feeling, even for a few days. The pursuits of pleasure, the euphoric feelings she got, and the highs she attained kept her happy for awhile. But, the lows were equally as low as the highs. When she felt good, it was only a temporary mask that covered the overwhelming emptiness she had.

She realized after several years of these pursuits–with

different men and various activities–that what was missing from the pleasure was a true, lasting joy–a joy that would not go away even when times were difficult and the inevitable setbacks and disappointments came. Without that foundation, without true joy, and without someone significant to share your life with, pleasure is temporary, selfish, and ultimately meaningless.

At the same time, she needed to be forgiven for all the wrong decisions she had made, for all the people, including herself, that she had hurt, and for all that she subjected herself to in her life up to that point. She wanted to start a new life. To do that, she needed to feel accepted again. She needed to feel she belonged to something bigger than herself– bigger, in fact, than anything this world could offer her. She needed to *feel* love–true, lasting love–and she needed to *be* loved–unconditionally. In accepting her groom when she finally agreed to go on this journey with him, she had all of that and more. But, that journey would come with a price.

~

It is days before Easter in the Middle East. At the time of writing this, I was in my office in Mahooz, Bahrain. Formally known as the Kingdom of Bahrain, it is a series of tiny islands on the western shore of the Persian Gulf. Bahrain is bordered and dwarfed by Saudi Arabia to the west. To the east-northeast, Iran is about 150 miles across the Gulf. Kuwait and Iraq are just a couple hundred miles up the border of Saudi Arabia to the north-northwest.

You see, over 30 years ago, I met and married Michael Lindsay, a man who became my teammate in this adventure here on Earth. Mike got a job over in Bahrain several years ago. During that time, he visited me in the States, and I went to live with him for part of the year. Although we spoke every day and communicated online via video often, it was a long distance relationship during those years, but we made it work. Since that time, we closed that chapter of our lives, by the grace of God, and

Michael is back in the States with me again. He is my husband in this life, and I am forever grateful that God put us together as a ministry team.

But, this book is not about that love story or even that ministry, important as they both are. It's about the bigger love story that we all need to come to grips with, the one that provides that ultimate peace. Interesting I should be thinking about peace with what's going on in that other part of the world.

As I sat there in the real "middle" of the Middle East that is Bahrain, I was also thinking about something that may surprise many of you. In my travels in this area, there is no one I found yet that does not believe that Jesus Christ truly lived. They also seem to agree that he was the best of men. In fact, the Muslim faith also believes, as it has been told to me, that Jesus Christ will return for the faithful. What they don't believe is that Jesus Christ died on a cross. It is just incomprehensible to them. So, there is little here to remind me of the sacrifice that Jesus made–no physical signs or symbols, such as crosses or crucifixes, that are so common in other parts of the world.

It is far more acceptable for the people in Bahrain to believe that Jesus Christ was not nailed to the cross, but an imposter was–that Jesus was just taken into heaven without the sacrifice of His shed blood. I must tell you that if I could write this story, I would find this a far more acceptable choice. Good thing God wrote this story and not me.

My Life with God

My life with God would prove to be another adventure that I had never imagined. At that moment of pure desperation when I cried out to God at 25 years old, I had finally said yes to His "love covenant". He was always ready for me, but I had not been ready to be aligned with Him until that moment. Finally, I had found my true love! The desire to learn more about Him was compelling.

Spending time with Him proved to be what increased my love for Him. I did this by reading the user's guide we mentioned earlier. You know the same kind you get when you need to troubleshoot a computer device or understand how a new gadget or appliance operates? This guide was all about fixing my heart and understanding the One I loved.

Do you remember the first time you fell in love? You just couldn't get enough of that person. That's what happened to me. Specifically, it was when I discovered one particular section in our user's guide, chapter eight of Romans, that something changed inside of me. I didn't know the plan for my life, but, when I read that chapter and understood it, I knew there was one. Romans 8 deals with many foundational issues, including the freedom from condemnation we have as believers and as "children of God", as well as the hope and assistance we have through prayer, the Holy Spirit, God's love, and the ultimate sacrifice and triumph we share through Christ Himself.

There is one part of me, my sinful nature, that was to be kept in this plan in order for me to "live by the Spirit", as we are commanded in the Galatians scripture that starts this chapter. But, what does it really mean to have a "sinful nature", and how is someone to truly "live by the Spirit"? It's all about becoming free–free from the bondage of sin and death that we are under as human beings. This freedom comes only one way, through Christ Jesus, and it is defined by the "law of the Spirit" that Paul discusses in his letters to the Romans and the Galatians. However, this law is not about following church doctrine, customs, traditions, or other laws of man and religion. Our sinful nature prevents our freedom no matter how "religious" we become.

My Adventure

So my adventure began. I was learning daily about the differences between the life I had been living while looking for love and the one I had been created to be in love with. Finally, I began to find answers that I had been searching for. The more questions I had, the more answers I got. If I had the time, He had the answers. Imagine that!

A real love relationship began to develop between me and the one I decided to join with in His love covenant. Have you ever been told that you were loved before you knew the feeling that comes with being in love? All of your senses seem to become more alive. Sometimes in the natural world they can diminish with time. Not so in this love relationship between God and me.

Our unity increased as my mind began to be controlled by the Spirit. With it came "life and peace" (Romans 8:6), yet please don't take this to suggest it is without cost. Life by the Spirit means that I had to put to death the misdeeds of my body. Listen up!

So it is written: "The first man Adam became a living being"; the last Adam, a life-giving spirit. 1 Corinthians 15:45

For the perishable must clothe itself with the imperishable, and the mortal with immortality. 1 Corinthians 15:53

The first man, Adam, became a living being, created by God to enjoy his creation, have dominion over it, and live a free life in paradise with Him. However, when he broke God's commandment by eating the forbidden fruit and brought sin into the world, he noticed immediately his nakedness. Out of shame, he had a desire to be clothed as a covering. He became perishable. With sin, death was brought into the world. Adam and Eve are also representative of all men and women. We must strive to be clothed with the imperishable to ultimately produce in us one like the last Adam, a life-giving spirit (I Cor.15:45, 53). What is imperishable? That which doesn't die!

This "last Adam", of course, represents the resurrected Jesus Christ, as the new creation that we all aspire to when we are "born again" and have new life in Him. Like Christ, when we are joined with him, our spirit is immortal, imperishable, indestructible. We are to "clothe ourselves with Christ" (Romans 13:14). To "clothe" ourselves is a metaphor repeated over and over in the New Testament, commanding us to be fully covered in everything that Jesus represents, including "compassion, kindness, humility, gentleness, and patience" (Colossians 3:12).

However, in gathering these "garments" and trying on such "clothes", it is an arduous process. These clothes will not always "fit" us–in fact, sometimes they may be tight, ill-fitting, and uncomfortable. There may be a lot of suffering along the way as we try to wear these clothes. As 2 Corinthians 5 says it, "we groan and are burdened" during the process. Instead of wearing our old clothes and living in the "tent" that represents our worldly life and the burdens we have here on Earth, we long to be clothed in our "heavenly dwelling", the kingdom that God has promised us when we accept Him. He made us for this purpose.

Sometimes all I could hear was my groaning. Take note that the flesh does not approve of this purpose, and that was definitely true in my life. Sometimes that groaning was my earthly desires to do something other than what "living by the Spirit" is supposed to mean. When sin entered this world, it became a way to separate us from love. Why God allowed sin to enter the world is a topic for another book, but it's a fair question. Some of the answer is in the ability God has given us to choose to love Him. I believe the longing for this love is what I had my entire life, even if initially it wasn't for Him. I came to realize that without God, I would never find it on my own. How could I?

The opening verse of this chapter, Galatians 5:16, gives details on this "life by the spirit". It is worthy of printing here. My testimony affirms the truth found in the following words.

So I say, live by the Spirit, and you will not gratify the desires of the sinful nature. For the sinful nature desires what is contrary to the Spirit and the Spirit what is contrary to the sinful nature. Galatians 5:16-17

No wonder I was having so much difficulty finding love on my own. The basest desires of who we are as humans are the opposite of what the Spirit–the divine part of us that God breathed into Adam–strives for. Until we can rely on His strength and resist the temptation of those earthly indulgences, we will continue to wallow in that sinful nature and never rise above it.

The following words convicted my heart further.

The acts of the sinful nature are obvious: sexual immorality, impurity and debauchery; idolatry and witchcraft; hatred, discord, jealousy, fits of rage, selfish ambition, dissensions, factions and envy; drunkenness, orgies, and the like. Galatians 5:19-21

Unfortunately, I had no trouble identifying myself with my sinful nature described here. Maybe you don't either. This section concludes with a warning that held my attention. It's the kind of attention you want to get from a child you love when you see they are heading towards danger, and you want to protect them.

I warn you...that those who live like this will not inherit the kingdom of God. Galatians 5:21b

The eighth chapter of Romans became my window of enlightenment. I still believe that if you can hear the words found in this chapter of our guide that understanding the rest of the document becomes clearer. It begins with a promise.

Therefore, there is now no condemnation for those who are in Christ Jesus because through Christ Jesus the law of the Spirit set me free from the law of sin and death. Romans 8:1-2

Identifying me with acts of the sinful nature was necessary, but apparently guilt was not. Unlike some of the human relationships many of us experience, I was not burdened with guilt nor had long-lasting emotional scars from my experiences early in life. My new relationship helped me overcome all of that. I think I breathed a sigh of relief that helped me to love Him even more. He knew about my wretched existence and He loved me anyway. Oh, how I was falling head over heels in love! The deeper my heart searched for love, the more I wanted to become what I was created to be. I did not yet know what that was exactly, but I knew that I had found love and I was not going to stop pursuing it.

The Price for Love

God condemned sin. Hmmmm.... Sin became identifiable to me and, yes, God condemned it. Remember, once you are a part of this love covenant, He is faithful and forgiving. Still, love sacrificed to make this possible in my life. I couldn't ignore that price.

I have already declared that my way in life–the choices I was making on my own and the life I was leading–just didn't work. Please don't forget this because, if you do, then the importance of this love relationship loses value. I couldn't find love apart from God. What was expressed to me as "love", such as my previous romantic relationships, generally abandoned me somewhere along life's path.

Living up to someone else's standard of love did not complete me. Any other standard of love caused me to fall short of that "life by the Spirit" I was supposed to live by–the purpose God created me for. This purpose is set in stone in our guide. No one, and certainly not I, can rewrite that portion of the guide that defines that purpose–to become at once part of God's family and that bride of Christ by choosing the only true source of love I have ever known.

Here's what the guide tells us about Jesus when he went to that cross on Calvary.

He himself bore our sins in his body on the cross, so that we might die to sins and live for righteousness. 1 Peter 2:24

Praise be to the God and Father of our Lord Jesus Christ! In his great mercy he has given us new birth into a living hope through the resurrection of Jesus Christ from the dead. 1 Peter 1:3

Through Jesus's death and subsequent resurrection, we are not slaves to our sinful nature. Instead, we have that "living hope" and we have the ability to "live for righteousness"–by the Spirit! God loved you and me so much that, though this price was the ultimate cost to Him–the sacrifice of his Son–He was willing to pay it because that's how much He loved you and me! The price He paid for me to be united to Him cannot be outspent, outbid, or outpaid by anyone or anything else.

What kind of love is this? Who am I that He would love me so much? I'm somebody that matters to Him. Though I feel I am unworthy, He loves me anyway. I've settled this matter forever in my heart and mind. I accept now that I could never have commissioned such a price for anyone to pay for me, but that doesn't change the story. Jesus did die on that cross, and he did rise from the dead. Love never fails. On that day at Calvary, it didn't either!

Crying Out for Love

It is difficult to imagine, but His death in this world brought life to me–for he redeemed me and anyone else who accepts Him because he overcame death and conquered sin. The Spirit himself testifies with our (my) spirit that we are God's children. We who are led by the Spirit of God are the sons of God. And by Him we cry "Abba, Father" (Romans 8:14-16). That's exactly what happened to me. I was crying out and He confirmed His love for me in that moment.

For I am convinced that neither death nor life, neither angels nor demons, neither the present nor the future, nor any powers, neither height nor depth, nor anything else in all creation, will be able to separate us from the love of God that is in Christ Jesus our Lord. Romans 8: 37-39

In short, *nothing* can separate us from the love of God when we are united to Christ Jesus. Quite the promise, don't you think?

Chapter Four
Growing Up with Love

You gave me life and showed me kindness, and in your providence watched over my spirit. I Peter 2:25

The bride was brought back to reality by a loud wail coming from the crowd–it was the sound of a baby crying. It was a reminder that all walks of life have been invited to this wedding, though some were more active participants than others. The tears shed represent the joy and sorrow that is part of any event like this. It was also a reminder that, in many ways, this was like a rebirth for her as she was to start a new life with her husband-to-be, the man she was destined to be with and who would make her life complete. What an adventure it would be!

It wasn't quite time for her to walk the aisle, but she was getting impatient. As Tom Petty has sung, the waiting is the hardest part, and it was getting more difficult every minute. The nervous flutterings she felt in the pit of her stomach must surely be more like caterpillars than butterflies, as she felt her transformation was still to come as she joined her groom–a man seemingly without fault, without flaw, without stain–and began to live out her days with him for eternity. But, how could she ever measure up?

She stepped closer to the threshold and peeked around the corner where she would be walking to see the people who would be witnesses and participants in this event. It was a large room, and it was very crowded with so many people who have known her and

The Absence of Love

had influence on her life over the years. All of her brothers and sisters who she grew up with were there. Also present were many of her other relatives and all of her close friends whom she shared her heart with over the years, and they with her. Her parents, unfortunately, were not present–they had passed away long ago. She recognized several acquaintances, some she knew and others she didn't or couldn't remember, almost like they were attending simply as curious spectators.

Then, she noticed others there that she didn't expect at all. There were many she recognized but didn't remember inviting, and even those who did not have a good influence on her life–some, in fact, that were like strange onlookers and rubberneckers acting like they were about to witness a car wreck and wanted to get a close-up of the mangled bodies about to be rolled away on stretchers or worse. Their intentions were unknown to her–maybe it was morbid curiosity or maybe it was a feeling this marriage would ultimately fail.

Finally, there were those in attendance who likely didn't even agree with this impending union and some, she was afraid, that didn't like her, and, worse still, detested the man she was about to be married to. Why were they even here? The butterflies in her stomach started turning to razor blades.

~

Growing up is hard to do. Sounds like a corny song title (it was, if anyone remembers the 60's band Ginger and the Snaps), but it's so true. Growing up in the Spirit can be even more difficult. His ways are in opposition to our own. During much of my early years, it felt like everything was against me. At 25, I was a single parent raising two boys alone. But, the feeling was different. I wasn't losing heart. Why?

Though I had made many mistakes in life, the one thing I knew was that these children were not part of that. In fact, though I didn't care what people thought of me previously, I now found I really did care what they thought about my children. They were so precious to me! Let me relate to you one example of this.

As children so often do at bedtime, my eldest son, Troy, after being put down for the night, had many diversions to sleeping. All of them brought him out of the bedroom and down the hall to where I was sitting in the living room. There were the traditional things that beckon a child before falling to sleep: going to the bathroom, wanting a drink, etc. and this night seemed no different for him. After several attempts to see to it he was to go to sleep, I issued a warning: "Troy! If you get out of bed one more time, it better be important, or it is going to cost you your rear end!"

Unfortunately, even that threat did not keep my son in bed. I heard his tiny little footsteps once again coming down the hall. I cried out, "This better be important!" Still, the footsteps came in my direction.

Finally, this small child of four was on his knees in front of me saying, "I accepted Jesus Christ as my Lord and Savior today, and I did it for you too. Is that important enough"?

I'd like to tell you I was the one who had this privilege to lead my young son to the Lord, but it wasn't me. A bus ministry at a local church had come to the apartment complex we were living in to see if they could pick up the children on Sunday mornings and take them to Sunday school. Having been raised in the church myself, I had no objections to this training and had agreed to this transportation ministry. It wasn't the denomination I had been raised in, but each week when the bus came my children were on it.

Now what do I say to this young son who has declared with such purpose to me the importance of his last trip out of bed and down the hall? This hit my heart and soul with such impact. My heart soared with love in that moment. I'm reminded of a scripture.

You intended to harm me, but God intended it for good to accomplish what is now being done, the saving of many lives. So then, don't be afraid. I will provide for you and your children. And he reassured them and spoke kindly to them. Genesis 50:20-21

What seemed intended to harm me and had me thinking I couldn't control my own children and keep them in bed, God intended for good–the saving of my own child!

I don't remember anything else that happened that day, but I will never forget those beautiful innocent eyes of my precious Troy so assuredly hoping that what he had done for himself, he had also done for me. Now that's love! That's exactly what our heavenly Father did for us. I couldn't reject my son, and we hadn't rejected His Son, either.

Shortly after my eldest son asked the Lord into his heart, I visited the church where he and his brother were attending. That day, I rededicated my life to the Lord. I was growing up!

Counterfeit Love

The year was 1977. It seems a whole lifetime ago now. Divorced mothers in those days were still looked down upon. Here I was raising two young boys–alone–in Peoria, Illinois.

Growing up didn't mean that I was living life righteously–quite the contrary. Love of a man continued to evade me, though the love I shared with my sons was critical to my development and maturity. I knew now I would never be able to love a man if he did not love my children as much as I did. Who knew that was possible?

I was staying with my parents because my work–selling insurance–had taken me there. The Lord had provided miraculously for me financially. The children were in their own home with our live-in housekeeper. I began to take an interest in a potential husband only to discover that he was married. In my mind, he was the last possibility I had to love a man. I was despondent.

As it says in Zechariah 2:8, I am the apple of God's eye. I didn't know that then, but I do now. He delights in pleasing me. He certainly did one late night when I was working in my hometown.

A Man to Love

There was a diner nearby my mother's home. I had invited her to go with me for an ice cream sundae. She declined. It was that night when I met the man who would become my husband: Michael Lindsay. We are still happily married after 34 years.

It was love at first sight for my husband and me. What I didn't know was that it would become that for my sons as well. They fell in love with this man who would become their father, and he with them. As my story goes, there was also a daughter by his first marriage. The boys became his great love, and she became mine.

Within my first year of marriage on my birthday, I decided to ask my husband for a Bible. I can't remember why I asked for that gift. We were living in a hotel in Baton Rouge, Louisiana. My husband was working there in the construction field. So it began with his birthday gift to me, the Bible, that I began reading the Word in that hotel room.

In the beginning, I was curious about the book of Revelation, and sometimes we read it together. With some humor, we sat on the bed in the hotel reading strange words as we laughed. My husband has an affinity for words. He mixes meanings of words and letters to become something they were never intended to be. Somehow, this was incorporated in his sense of humor and the book of Revelation gave him plenty of fire power. Who knew the pleasantry that I would continue to get for years reading from the Bible, our very guide for this book?

God Speaks to Me

We didn't like much about that part of the world or my husband's job, so we headed out for a place called Kalkaska, Michigan, with another promise for work. Here's where I began to "hear" God speak to me.

"You should be eating meat," He said to me, "and you are

only able to drink milk." I wept. You might be asking: what in the world made me cry from that statement? It was because I knew exactly what He was saying to me. He wanted to talk to me in depth and I was just a baby. Oh, how I cried that day! I think it was a purifying cry, however, because my heart seemed to crave, from that day on, the deep things of God. I didn't know it, but God was birthing in me "spiritual meat" to prepare me for the purpose I had been created for by Him.

For better or worse, our families were now bound together–my husband's, mine, and–yet unknown to us–ours. My husband became the love of my life just as I had hoped for in 1963 when I was telling God I was looking for love. In the beginning, I used to tell my husband everything about my experiences and what I learned in my Bible study, but soon my time with the Lord became very intense. I remember telling my husband that I could no longer share everything that was happening to me daily as there were not enough hours in the day. At that time, I was studying the Bible several hours a day. I was changing, but I wasn't sure whether my husband was.

Be Holy

What holds a family together? Most would probably answer "love", but few would know what that meant, and I was among the majority. My definition of love was changing daily as my experience with Him became stronger.

We all have demands we put on our relationships. They're not all pure demands either. In fact, if most of us are honest, purity is not the goal we seek in our relationships. That's because sin taints us. No matter how good we are, our innocence, our goodness (and the not-so-nice qualities in our lives) must be made "holy".

But just as he who called you is holy, so be holy in all you do; for it is written: "Be holy, because I am holy." 1 Peter 1:15-16

In order for us to truly serve God on the basis of love, our guide tells us that we must be "holy". But, what does that really mean?

When Peter writes "it is written", he is referring to the book of Leviticus in the Old Testament. In chapters 11 and 19 of Leviticus, God tells Israel to be "holy", by which He means for them to be different from the other nations by giving them specific rules to govern their lives. Israel is God's chosen people, set apart from all other groups at that time. God gave these special people certain standards to live by so the world would know they belonged to Him.

When Peter refers to the Lord's words in 1 Peter 1:16, he is speaking to believers. Believers need to be "set apart" from the world. They are being asked to live by God's standards, not the world's. God isn't calling those who believe in Him to be perfect, but to be distinct from the world. That's what he means to "become holy". And, that's what was starting to happen to me.

My husband was encouraging to me, though he continued on his own path. This would eventually put strain on our relationship, but let's not get ahead of my story. For a season, our love and His grace continued to live in one household in peace and harmony.

I had a lot of questions; and each day of study answered another and another. Once I understood there was another way to live–life by the spirit–I wanted to know everything about it. For me, there was a great deal to learn. Selfishness was still a part of my soul, though, so it wasn't going to be easy for me.

Speaking of "holy", it was the Holy Spirit, I soon learned from John 14:46, our "advocate", who was more than able to "teach me all things". However, some of these things–compassion, kindness, humility, gentleness and long suffering–were not things I wanted to sign up for. Really!

Putting On Love

In studying Colossians 3:12-14, I learned about the qualities that God desires us to have, including the characteristics

The Absence of Love

just mentioned. It also says "...over all these virtues put on love, which binds them all together." My love was nowhere near ready to encompass this.

What binds a family together? The simple answer, again, is love. But, what kind of qualities, distinctive characteristics, and uniqueness would love try to bind together in our family?

Thankfully, true love accepts you right where you are. It would just simply be wrong to think it leaves you the same way. The body has ligaments. The operative or active letter in this word is the "s" that holds it together. Apparently, there were virtues that did the same kind of work in me. Love was something "put on" over compassion, kindness, humility, gentleness, and long suffering. What kind of package were we? What were we trying to bind together? Let's find out!

Chapter Five
The Fruits of the Spirit

For the harvest of the earth is ripe. I Peter 2:25

The bride had been peeking around the corner of the aisle, having all these conflicting emotions as she realized the union that was about to take place and all the witnesses, pro and con, to this event. She suddenly became aware of a sensation she was feeling–a physical sensation. It was a gentle tap on the shoulder. At first, she thought she was imagining it, but then she felt it again–two fingers directly on her right shoulder. Tap. Tap. She turned around.

She was pleased to see one of her best friends in the world, Lily, the wedding coordinator. But, she was much more than that. Lily wasn't related to the groom, but you would have thought the two of them were brother and sister. The resemblance was uncanny, as if they had the same parents. Lily had known the groom for many years, early in the bride's life, as their families attended some of the same charity functions and hung out in the same social circles.

Earlier in her life, the bride also was at some of these events, but never when the groom was present. Lily had opportunity to introduce the bride to the groom on numerous occasions, but she later told the bride the timing wasn't right for such a meeting. Lily and the groom never had any romantic attachment themselves. Their relationship was always one of respect and mutual admiration for their humanitarian endeavors, and they worked very well together. The groom tended to lead in an active role, going into the rough areas of the town or country where their efforts led them and tackling the situation head on. Lily's role was more as a helper and a cheerleader, always encouraging others to join in their causes and prompting others to take action.

Years ago, the bride met Lily at a fund raising event at a college where they were both helping to gather food and money for a homeless shelter. Lily was always so patient and kind with the bride, even during the roughest times of her life and when she was at her lowest. She was also a great counselor, and was equally as good at admonishment when it was called for, but it was always in a straight-forward yet gentle way, so the message was loud and clear, and easily received. The bride needed that kind of talking to on many occasions, and Lily always had a way of putting things so her words dug deep at whatever issue was troubling the bride. It was at this moment, with the bride standing at the threshold and swirling with emotion, that Lily spoke, and it was what the bride needed to hear right then. It was always that way with her.

"Just a few more minutes," Lily said, with the sweetest tone the bride had ever heard.

"Yes," was all the bride could manage as a response. She began to cry.

"You are a beautiful bride," Lily added, with true joy in her voice. "You two will make an awesome couple. I am so happy for you and so glad to be with you on your wedding day. I love you!"

"Thank you, Lily. I love you too! You are the best friend any girl could have."

"You are about to *marry* your best friend. But, thank you for that."

Of course, she was right. Her groom had become her best friend, as well as her romantic soul mate. But, it was her relationship with Lily that had taught her so much in the areas where she lacked, she couldn't help complimenting her in that way. Lily had a joy to life that she longed for, a peacefulness that always put everyone at ease, and was faithful to her causes and the people whom she called friends. She was such a role model for the bride–so loving, so kind, so patient. Yet, Lily was also a spitfire–feisty, spirited, wild, and free. She was also the toughest girl the bride had ever known.

That was way more than the bride could say about herself, but at least she had finally matured enough to see where she fell behind in those areas and where she needed to grow and develop. She realized that, though she had definitely improved in her confidence, courage, and self-worth, she could never simply rely on her own power and strength. Instead, she would always lean on Lily and the groom to get her out of the toughest binds that life wrapped her up in.

She thought back to one night, many years ago, when it wasn't simply a rough spot she found herself in. She was in fear for her life.

~

When a seed is planted, it bears like fruit. In Chapter 1, we studied about "the beginning". We learned that the land produced vegetation, plants bearing seed according to their kinds. Though our guide was addressing vegetation, we are going to discover that it is not so different for us. The sinful nature of man produces like kind and I had come to learn that "spirit" man, which we take on and develop when we become followers of Christ, does as well.

When we accept Jesus and truly have that desire to follow Him, it is like a seed planted in us that can grow to be a great tree, bearing the most delectable fruit you have ever tasted. As a tree is fertilized, properly pruned, and cared for, it will continue to bear much fruit. But, like a tree that is neglected, so too a persons' heart could turn away from God when that sinful nature, like excessive weeds or fungus, is allowed to take over the life of the tree.

God sent the Holy Spirit, the third person of the trinity, to "sanctify" us by providing a way for us to become "holy" and giving life and breath to His church and its people. This "spirit" lives in us as humans, just as much as our soul and our body, and

The Absence of Love

does battle with our sinful nature to nurture our spiritual growth.

In his letter to the Galatians, Paul describes nine attributes or "fruits" that are outward signs of that growth and development in this sanctification process. These fruits, which grow from seeds when we first accept Christ as Savior, are a way for us to be transformed into the image of Christ that He wants us to be. It is by the power of the Holy Spirit that this process is done in your life. You have to be willing to work in cooperation with the Holy Spirit. These "fruits of the spirit" will be dealt with individually in chapters of each. 1 will name all nine of them here, and will discuss them in a little different order in the chapters that follow.

According to Galatians 5:22-23, the fruits of the spirit are:

1. Love
2. Joy
3. Peace
4. Forbearance (patience)
5. Kindness
6. Goodness
7. Faithfulness
8. Meekness (gentleness)
9. Temperance (self-control)

After listing these fruits, Paul ends this passage with a curious statement:

Against such things there is no law. Those who belong to Christ Jesus have crucified the sinful nature with its passions and desires. Since we live by the Spirit, let us keep in step with the Spirit. Galatians 5:23b-25

What does Paul mean by "against such things there is no law"? He is not saying we should ignore the laws of man, or that bearing these fruits makes law unnecessary. As He says in Matthew 5:17, Jesus did not come to abolish the law, but to fulfill it. Until our righteousness surpasses that of the teachers of the law, we will not "enter the kingdom of heaven".

To become righteous and holy (or "sanctified"), Paul is saying that we are to deal with others in a similar way that God has dealt with us–with all nine fruits operating in full effect. Like Jesus being crucified on the cross, we can "crucify our own sinful nature" by "belonging to Christ" and "living by the spirit". Additionally, God gave us what we don't deserve, and we are therefore to give others what they don't deserve. God didn't deal with us on the basis of law, but on the basis of His love and that love covenant He made with us from the very beginning. We must therefore deal with others using those same attributes of love, joy, peace, patience, kindness, goodness, faithfulness, gentleness, and self-control.

The fruits of the spirit are required to produce proper responses to God. It is important to understand that we are not able to be "good enough" on our own to produce these fruits. The fruits of the spirit require the active participation and interaction of our hearts with God. Apart from this interaction, fake fruits engulf and entangle us, allowing deception to further weigh us down, exacting an opposite effect caused by the nine fruits of the spirit in our lives.

As I am typing this, I am sitting again in the Middle East. Especially in a place like this, it seems a difficult task to accomplish a truly mature relationship with the Lord. Rules and regulations of purity are visible all over this area. I see random acts of kindness rejected, and my heart aches. My eldest son stretches out his hand of fellowship to greet a woman in Bahrain visiting in our home. She responds by withdrawing her hand from touching his! (This happens to Muslim men as well.) Our son is an extension of the kindness that is Christ Jesus in this place. Her learned reaction is to pull away from such kindness.

I share this brief story because the mask to become kind apart from Christ must be removed. According to Romans 8:7, our sinful nature is in "enmity" (a mutual hatred or ill will) or "hostile" to God. We are not able, apart from God, to know "good" from "evil". We are unequipped and unable to do so since sin entered the world. However, we have hope, and that is through our relationship with the Holy Spirit.

Developing Character

This is an introduction to the importance and relevance of the nine fruits of the spirit. Maturity as sons and daughters of Him does not occur without the development of these fruits in our lives. If they are non-apparent in our lives, the natural man will understand something is lacking. The spiritual man should prepare his soul to be enhanced by pursuing the fruits of the spirit. The Lord will begin instruction right where you are through the circumstances of your life.

Our character must be shaped by conforming to His likeness through the power of His most Holy Spirit. Christ Jesus recognized that, in and of our own human nature, this transformation is impossible. However, a way has been provided by our heavenly Father to accomplish His divine nature in us. Believing in Jesus and inviting him into our heart is the greatest gift of love, and it's an essential starting point in our Christian walk. However, depending on it alone to bring peace is not confirmed in the scriptures. We are to grow in the characteristics of His divine nature and build upon the foundation of our salvation by way of these "fruits of the spirit".

Fruits and Seeds

Webster's definition of fruit in part is an edible reproductive body of a seed plant: one having a sweet pulp associated with the seed (the fruit of the tree), or the effect or consequence of an action, such as a product or result.

By definition, fruit is affected by the consequences of an action. The desired result, of the fruits of the spirit, produces the effect of a correct response to God.

A seed, by definition, is sown, producing offspring. Of course, this includes the male sperm, which unites with the female egg to produce the physical man. However, all seeds do not produce sweet pulp. I didn't! My selfish, sinful nature was still alive and kicking in me. However, maturity was in the making, but it would take more time spent with love in our guide.

Chapter Six
Love – A Fruit of the Spirit

There is no fear in love. But perfect love drives out fear.
1 John 4:18

It was many years ago, but the bride's memory of that night was as vivid as if it had been yesterday. She was attending the party of an acquaintance at work. Everyone from the office was invited, and many came. It was getting very late and the party was long over, but the remaining guests didn't seem to notice.

The drinks had been flowing, and so were the emotions of those still up and about. It was always interesting to the bride to see how various people handled their alcohol. On this night, most didn't very well. Some were incoherent, others silly and giggly, and still others were getting angry and upset. Some had simply passed out on the couches, chairs, and love seats spread throughout the spacious mansion. The host and hostess were nowhere in sight. The bride assumed they had either retired to a back bedroom to engage in who knows what with who knows who else, or had left the madness altogether, maybe to hit a night club somewhere downtown–there were many to choose from.

She knew she was in no condition to drive, but she was too drunk to make the best decision either. A co-worker and close friend of the host named Stan noticed her predicament, and moved in to take full advantage of it.

"Hey, you know you can't drive home," Stan said.

"Yeah, I know…" she managed, "but I've got to get home. I've got things I have to do in the morning."

There was a pregnant pause as they stared at each other. The bride was going through a very rough time at this stage in her life. Her boss was becoming more demanding, and she couldn't seem to keep up with all her bills, despite working overtime most weeks. She was depressed. She knew she had friends she could rely on for comfort and advice, but she tended to stay away from most of them lately, because they also always had that tough-love counsel for her that she didn't want to hear. Particularly her best friend, Lily. Ugh. She didn't want to hear what she would say at this moment, but she knew Lily would not be smiling right now.

"Well, I could drive you home in your car," he offered. "I took a taxi here because I figured I'd be in your condition too, but I'm really not too bad. I'll just take a taxi home from there."

She knew she shouldn't have said anything but "No thank you", but he seemed like a nice guy and those were hard to come by these days. She knew Stan worked in the same department, but she had minimal interaction with him at the firm–nothing more than a good morning or hello. Sometimes she did notice him when he walked past her or when he was talking to friends. She didn't know him at all, but maybe this was her opportunity to get to know him a little better. Besides, he was good-looking, he was smart, and he did seem to be genuinely concerned about her condition. Maybe this could be the start of something good, she thought. Love comes in all kinds of disguises, and can sometimes sneak up on you when you least expect it. Maybe this was the case here.

"Sure, you can drive me home. I only live about 10 minutes from here."

~

One fruit of the spirit is love. It's not just ordinary love either. The Greek word used for this kind of love is "agape", which is referenced several other times in the New Testament. It is the kind of love described when addressing holy living. such as in

Colossians 3:12-15, in which we are commanded to "put on love" over certain virtues (compassion, kindness, humility, gentleness, and patience). It is this agape love that "binds these virtues together in perfect unity".

Love is considered the "greatest" of the only three things that "remain", exceeding even "faith and hope" (1 Corinthians 13:13). Love is also "the most excellent way" (1 Cor. 12:31) when Paul is describing the gifts of the Holy Spirit, such as prophecy and speaking in tongues. He says that even if someone is speaking in the tongues of "angels", yet does not have love, "he is like a resounding gong or clanging cymbal" (1 Cor. 13:1). In other words, it's like someone who makes a lot of noise and draws much attention to themselves, lacking the foundation of that true, selfless love that we all need to make any of the spiritual "gifts" mean something more than simply a loud spectacle.

Jesus Himself speaks of the importance of agape love when he says emphatically "Love the Lord your God with all your heart and with all your soul and with all your mind" (Matthew 22:37-40). We need to put forth all the effort of our being in loving our God. It's what He deserves and what we are commanded to do, yet that love is still a choice.

John 3:16

Then, there is the "salvation" verse, cited when someone wants to deliver the Gospel message in one verse:

For God so loved the world that he gave his only begotten son that whosoever believeth in him would not perish, but have life everlasting. John 3:16

It's quite possibly the most famous scripture in the Bible. It's been held up for decades on signs at ball games, imprinted in full color on billboards, advertised on church bulletin boards, and yelled out by street preachers to any passers by within earshot. It was the last scripture NFL quarterback Tim Tebow wore in his "eye black" (the grease that ball players apply under the eye to reduce glare from the sun or stadium lights) while playing in his senior year for the University of Florida before messages in the eye black of any kind were banned by the NCAA. Whole books have been written on this verse. But, what does it really mean?

In a nutshell, John is saying that, when we truly believe in Jesus Christ and accept Him as personal Lord and Savior, although we will suffer a physical death, our soul will live forever in his presence when we make it into heaven. But, it is in that sacrifice of His one and only son–Himself in human form–that God shows us how much He loves us. In doing so, the chains of sin that bind us have been cut loose, setting us free.

This kind of sacrificial love holds similar characteristics to that found in the book of Galatians, as in the mention of love as the first fruit of the spirit (Chapter 5:22) and when Paul says in Chapter 2 that "I live by faith in the Son of God, who loved me and gave himself for me."

The Love Passage

Of course, there is also "the" love passage, found in First Corinthians, in which the apostle Paul waxes poetic on the idea of agape love and provides a succinct definition in probably the most famous love poem in scripture.

Love is patient, love is kind. It does not envy, it does not boast, it is not proud. It does not dishonor others, it is not self-seeking, it is not easily angered, it keeps no record of wrongs. Love does not delight in evil but rejoices with the truth. It always protects, always trusts, always hopes, always perseveres. Love never fails. 1 Corinthians 13:4-8a

In this simple, direct description of the virtues of love, Paul captures much of what is also part of the nine "fruits of the spirit", including patience, kindness, and faithfulness (trust and hope), while providing several more attributes to expand the definition of agape love from a biblical perspective.

John the Beloved Disciple

In the first letter of John, the apostle asks us to "love one another, for love comes from God." He continues by offering an even simpler definition of love in Chapter 4 Verse 10: "This is love: not that we loved God, but that he loved us and sent his Son as an atoning sacrifice for our sins." In this case, it's not about us loving Him, but that He loved us. It's why the world and everyone who has ever lived even exists–simply, because of His "love". Many Biblical scholars agree that John himself is regarded as the "beloved" disciple, the one whom "Jesus loved" (John 21:20), even though this disciple is not mentioned by name in regard to this title.

Galatians Love

In the "love" described in Galatians, love is an expression of "true faith" (Gal 5:6). We also have the "freedom to serve one another in love" (Gal 5:13). At the same time, when we make the point and focus of that faith to be in Jesus Christ, our Lord and God who first loved us, we are motivated to love others in the same way.

That, of course, is easier said than done, considering the battle we have every day with our sinful nature as we work toward eventually becoming that beautiful "bride of Christ". It was definitely not easy for me. Let's revisit my personal story to see all this discussion from one person's practical viewpoint.

Deciding to Love

I had been looking for "love" for much of my early years without much success. When affection came to me in the form of a potential human mate, of course I hoped this would be the "love of my life". What I did not know early on was that, apart from God I can do nothing, including giving love or feeling love, in any true, meaningful sense. There had clearly been an absence of love in my life. Let's remember that love became a choice "in the beginning". We cannot forget where we have come from on this journey. I decided to love God in my life and that love covenant engaged His faithfulness and mercy. This is the seed sown in me, before the fruit of love matures.

Without God's participation in my life, love would prove to be evasive. Even with God in my life, I had to learn another way. My ways developed over time, and I was about to find out that it can take time for His ways to develop in me as well. Love had been decided upon in my life, and would remain my motivation to continue to overcome the challenges that time would bring me.

Family Under Construction

It's now 1985. I'm on my way to the doctor. My husband and two sons are living with me on four acres in Shady Hills, Florida. We are living in an eighteen-foot travel trailer, preparing the land to build our new home. I'm not certain, but, looking back, I think hard work is a part of love because I was mowing that four acres myself with a push lawn mower.

On this particular day, my time was spent going to visit the doctor. I know I hadn't been feeling well, but I was not prepared for what the doctor was going to tell me.

Our youngest son, Todd, was now twelve years old. That means my husband and I have now been married for seven years. It also means I was thirty-five years old.

It never occurred to me on the way to visit the doctor that he was going to tell me that I was pregnant. Honestly, I was shocked! We had decided that if I did not get pregnant by the time I was thirty-six that we would not consider having a child because of the health risks–both for the child and me. It just didn't occur to me that the symptoms I had were that of a new visitor (the permanent kind) preparing to come into our lives. Well, love found a way. On the trip home from the doctor, I needed windshield wipers on my eyes because I was crying so much.

I'm not sure, but I think my husband was as surprised as me when I told him. We packed up our belongings and headed back to the small home we already owned in Zephyrhills, Florida. The building of a larger home would have to wait. Right now, we were going into a different kind of construction and my energy would have to be focused completely on preparing for this new life to emerge.

Appear he did! When coming into view, it became apparent that love would expand each one of us. We were all going to grow up in love. Looking at this precious, new-born child, whom we named Christopher, it brought love unanimously into the lives of our children, my husband, and me. Everyone was enamored with him.

The Twelve Tribes

On the day of Christopher's baby dedication, our daughter Christy decided that she wanted to redirect her life and help take care of her newborn baby brother. His home was where the laundry room used to be. The other two boys, Troy and Todd, shared a bedroom. With no other space available and no time to build, the arrival of our baby boy meant a larger home would be needed. Our family was growing and our love was expanding.

Now there were three children–ages twelve, thirteen, and fourteen–living under one roof with their baby brother. Christopher seemed to bring peace to our family. There was plenty of room in each of our hearts for him and we all enjoyed the years that would come watching the unity he brought to our family, which we started calling the "twelve tribes of Israel", even though there were only six of us. Needless to say, our genealogy would make an unusual-looking family tree. But no matter! We were happy and love was connecting us in ways we could not have imagined.

Our family became my podium. What I learned from the

guide, I was passing on daily to them.

Todd, our middle child, seemed to be looking for love in all the wrong places too, so he got the best of my real-life sermons. Troy, our eldest son, led a life that gave him the nickname Mr. Responsible. He wanted a car at sixteen, so off to work he went. Between school, soccer, and work, he often became invisible. Our talks often took place while I was hanging clothes on the line. His understanding of my challenges, whatever they were, allowed us to develop a deep connection. We were especially close.

Our daughter Christy, after moving in with us full time, began to look for love too. She is a beautiful girl, so finding love (or at least affection) wasn't a problem for her. She got plenty of attention from the opposite sex. However, her dilemma was in determining the source of that love. Together, it would prove to be one of our most difficult challenges in life.

These kids were all teenagers at the same time, so defining love was a full-time occupation for our family.

Making More Noise

We were now all regulars at church. When we were home, our life continued to develop spiritually because I was well on my way to learning about life by the spirit. Sometimes I was that "resounding gong or clanging cymbal" that we discussed earlier from 1 Corinthians 13 – making a lot of noise and drawing a lot of attention to myself, but lacking in true love. That verse continues with this:

If I have the gift of prophecy and can fathom all mysteries and all knowledge, and I have a faith that can move mountains, but have not love, I am nothing. If I give all I possess to the poor and surrender my body to the flames, but have not love, I gain nothing. 1 Cor: 13:1

Paul is saying here that, even if we have these powerful, spiritual gifts, even if we have enormous faith, we still need that foundational love or it is all for naught. It is very easy to begin to think you are becoming some kind of authority, particularly when those spiritual gifts become apparent and that great faith manifests itself, as it did in me. It was difficult to comprehend because I was trying so hard to follow the guide. I was seeking with all my heart to become like our Savior and live the life that Jesus would want me to live. In reality, I often was more like that gong or cymbal, an obnoxious noisemaker. As Romans 3:23 says, we all "fall short of the glory of God", and I think I fell short of the mark much of the time.

Still my family knew I was on the right path, and thank God they loved me, errors and all. I think this is important to know as a parent. We make mistakes even when we are reading and trying our best to follow the user's guide!

Building a Life

I began to feel a bit like a rudder on a ship. It doesn't take long as a parent with three teenagers to realize you are not in control. This worked well for me in that love was trying to teach me this too. My kids were not the only ones growing up.

Here I remember relating very strongly to Amos, a book included in our guide in the Old Testament. He didn't call it a rudder, but a plumb line. A plumb line, I learned later, was a string with a metal weight at one end that, when suspended, points directly towards the earth's center of gravity and makes a right angle to the ground. It's used to make a straight vertical line and can be used to determine the depth of water. My husband was a plumber, but at the time I didn't have a clue what anything having to do with plumbing meant.

Here's what it says in Amos:

*This is what He showed me: The Lord was standing by a wall that had been built true to plumb, with a plumb line in his hand. And the Lord asked me, "What do you see, Amos?" A plumb line, I replied. Then the Lord said, "Look, **I am** setting a plumb line* *among my people... Amos 7:7-8*

When we devote our lives to pursuing Him, we can have that direct vertical relationship with God as our plumb line. We need to direct our path straight at Him and plant our feet on solid ground at a right angle so that we are as aligned to His plumb line as much as possible.

Our guide often uses construction terms and concepts when addressing our lives. Love was building in me a place that God himself would reside. Asking Jesus in my heart had happened a long time ago, and that is the foundation of the building–it's like laying your life on solid rock. Any other foundation, I learned, was "sinking sand". Jesus uses these metaphors in Matthew 7:24-27 of our guide where he describes the "wise man who built his house on the rock." The wind and rain cannot wash it away. But, he continues, the "foolish man builds his house on sand," which comes falling down with a "great crash" when the wind and rains come beating against it. I definitely had my share of wind and rain, and, although I had that solid rock foundation, I still had a way to go for the construction in my life to be completed.

Feeling Rejected

There were the normal issues people have raising a family, and differences between my husband and me, but then to my surprise there was another building zone in my life that wasn't going well–the Church. This was difficult for me to understand because I was reading the guide and applying it to my life. Even stranger was finding that sharing the knowledge of what I was learning seemed to stir people up.

I haven't told you much about my relationship with my mother growing up. To describe my feelings in one word, it would be "rejected". Most of us can relate to feeling rejected by the world, and I had that too, so, for me, being rejected by my mother was strike number two. Rejection was taking a stronghold in my life. When this continued into the Church, well...that was really unnerving. The more I spoke about what I was learning, the more I received the left hand of fellowship. I could serve, but I couldn't lead! After ten years of this kind of fellowship, I pressed into love even harder.

The book of Amos taught me that just because you go to church doesn't mean you are worshiping God. It could be one was merely participating in ceremony or ritual, which falls short of true worship. God wants our hearts and He wants our simple trust in Him–not showy, external actions. He wants heartfelt obedience and commitment.

Walking through the halls of the church we attended, I remember fully engaging God with my frustrations. Clearly I heard Him say, "You asked for my power–now learn to walk in it!" Yikes! Love was going to require my submission in a lot of places that I would have otherwise resisted, but His plumb line would not be moved in me. I was confronted often with my own shortcomings, but there were many other times that He would have me be silent, or do nothing at all, even when error was obvious.

Getting Irritated in Bible Study

During adult vacation Bible school, our Pastor was leading the class. He was discussing the apostle Paul and wondering why we, the class, thought Paul was so successful everywhere he went. I was astonished. Everywhere he went?

I knew from the guide that Paul had been shipwrecked, snake bitten, and, for two years, was imprisoned without a trial. For much of his early ministry after he had his conversion experience on the road to Damascus and changed his name from Saul, Paul's reception was not good much of the time. However, the class began to respond about Paul's education, and his ability to speak well to communicate with people. I believed they were missing the point. Sure, he had success in Corinth in building a church, but that was after many failed attempts in Philippi, Thessolinica, Berea, and Athens! When he went to Corinth, he was miserable and depressed. Fortunately, his legacy changed, and through his failures, he learned how to speak to the unsaved and minister to them. But, you can't talk about Paul without talking about his struggles.

The more the class spoke about how wonderful Paul's ministry was, the more irritated I became. Yet, the Lord shut my mouth and would not let me respond. I was quite upset by the time I arrived home and spent a great deal of this frustration with the Lord one-on-one. His response surprised me further. He said, "If you go to battle in this place, it would be an ambush to your soul. It would engage you in a battle I never intended for you. It would keep you from My heart." Love once again found a way in me.

The Husbandman/Bridegroom

Though I have spent a great deal of time thus far sharing my story with love, it is only the reflection of a much larger love chronicle. The word "husbandman" is an old Middle English term translated from the original Greek word of "georgos" (from which we derive the English first name of George, by the way). The word refers to a farmer or one who plows or cultivates a field or vineyard and takes care of and has dominion over the animals. It's where we derive our modern word for the male spouse–husband. The emphasis is on the work that needs to be done after the marriage happens–the role that the male plays in providing for the family, just as God is our "great provider" who ultimately fulfills all our needs and, through the Holy Spirit, cultivates our spiritual growth by the "fruits of the spirit".

In our guide, the concept of "husbandman" is mentioned several times in the Old and New Testament. For example, in John 15:1, he likens us to branches and he to the "vine" and his Father to the "husbandman." Apart from the vine, the branches would wither and die. Yet, we as the Church are that vineyard that is cultivated, and God is the husbandman that is Lord over us. But, there's a romantic element in scripture to the concept of the husband or groom who is joined to the wife or bride in marriage, particularly in the Old Testament.

In Isaiah 61:10, Israel is likened to the bride, and God to the husbandman or bridegroom ready to take His bride clothed in the "garments of salvation" and covered with the "robe of righteousness". God is the groom "adorning his head like a priest", and the church is the bride "adorning her head with jewels."

Book of Hosea

Then, there is the sequence of events related in the Book of Hosea. Hosea, first in the order of the twelve minor prophets in the Old Testament, prophesied during a dark time of Jewish history, around 800 BC. Most of the people at that time had turned away from God, and worshipped the calves of Jereboam and Baal, a Canaanite God.

In Hosea 2, God speaks to Israel, while referencing Hosea's own wife and children. He tells of how God's people must turn away from sin, and threatens them with all levels of punishment for their idolatry of Baal. But, he also talks of the restoration that will happen when the bridegroom/husbandman is betrothed to His church, the bride:

I will betroth you to me forever; I will betroth you in righteousness and justice, in love and compassion. I will betroth you in faithfulness, and you will acknowledge the Lord. Hosea 2:19-20

God's betrothal comes to us in faithfulness once again. I liken this to the love covenant because His faithfulness to us is what seals the relationship of love. God will bind us to Himself forever. The husbandman used Hosea to tell us of His great love for us.

We will most assuredly fall from grace somewhere in this world, but we are assured His great compassion will draw us back to this vast love. His wonderful grace and compassionate mercy is His wedding gift to us. Though we are undeserving of it and have done nothing to earn it, His forgiveness knows no bounds.

I wanted to know more about this "husbandman" in Hosea.

The Absence of Love

As mentioned already, a husbandman is a land worker or a farmer. Being from the Midwest, I knew something about farming. In fact, in my younger years, going to my Aunt and Uncle's farm was one of my favorite things to do. There were hay lofts of which we built long tunnels through. A creek flowed through their property and under a small bridge. My cousins and I would hide there. They had milking cows and chickens and acres and acres of property where we could run and play for hours. It was easy for me to connect "love" to the idea of a husbandman or farmer!

Now I wanted to know more about Him. The prophet Isaiah helped me learn more.

Before me no God was formed, nor will there be one after me. I, even, I am the Lord, and apart from me there is no savior. I have revealed and saved and proclaimed. Isa 43:10-12

Even to your old age and gray hairs I am he, I am he who sustains you. I have made you and I will carry you; I will sustain you! I will rescue you. Isa 46:4

For your maker is your husband. The Lord almighty is his name. Isa 54:5

Love was expounding to me line upon line from our guide. I knew I was developing truth in my inner being, in my heart—something I had long desired. But, it is clear that what happens next has much less to do with me than Him.

Chapter Seven
Joy

Enter through into the joy of the Lord. Matthew 25:21

The bride walked out of the spacious home, led by Stan, who acted quite the gentleman. He took her arm as they strolled along the front walkway toward the cars parked along the street. She found herself having to lean on him a little, which she really didn't want to do, but she had no choice–she would have fallen over otherwise. Sure, he was a little buzzed, but she was definitely past the point of being able to drive safely.

"Which one is yours?" he asked with a kindness in his voice that startled her.

"The silver one there," she said, pointing to a sporty Jaguar XK super-charged V8 parked a couple cars away to the right under a bright street lamp.

"Wow, a jag. Nice!" he said.

"Thanks....yeah, I like it," was her response. She actually was starting to feel pretty good about herself. She was relieved she didn't have to drive home and a nice guy was driving her. She liked being taken care of. And all guys just loved her car.

"Do you have the keys?" he asked.

"Yeah. But you don't need them."

"What? I thought I was driving."

"You are."

As they approached the car, the Jaguar unlocked itself

The Absence of Love

without any motion by her. They walked around to the passenger side and he opened the door, made sure she got inside safely, then closed it gently.

True to form, he walked around the front of the car and stopped to admire the hood and front grill. He looked up at her and their eyes met for a second, and they both smiled at each other. As he continued looking at the front of the car, she admired his taste. He had on a black dress shirt that was partially tucked inside a pair of dressy blue jeans, with a black and silver belt. A pair of snakeskin boots and what appeared to be a Rolex on his wrist finished the ensemble. He had dark hair, bright blue eyes, a chiseled, slightly unshaven jaw, and a gently muscular build–all things she liked.

He opened the driver door and hopped in. He looked around the inside a little bit, running his hand over the steering wheel and then over the top of the dashboard as he turned to her and smiled again.

"Quite a car. Considering you are a single woman. What is this–an 8-cylinder, like 400 horsepower?" he guessed.

"Something like that," she said, as she adjusted her seatbelt. It was actually a 510 horse, but who was counting? She saw that he didn't realize, or pretended not to realize, how to start the car. She motioned to the red, pulsating start button.

"Gotcha," he said, as he pressed it. You could tell he was comfortable behind a car like this, but the bride thought he was trying to play dumb and vulnerable. His dishonesty was sweet in a weird way and made him even more attractive. He practically jumped when the engine fired up, the vents auto-opened, and the dashboard display lit up like blue Christmas lights. She chuckled at his reaction. The stainless steel shift dial rose up from the center console. He looked down and to his right, first at her legs, and then at the shift dial. He placed his hand on it and shifted into gear, trying to act as cool as possible.

"Which way?" he asked.

"Turn left here, and I'll tell you from there."

"You could just tell me the address. I know the south side of town pretty well. This was my old stomping grounds. Still is, to some degree."

"Oh really? Well, I just moved here a year ago, to be closer to work. I'm still trying to find my way around town here."

"So, what's your address?"

She hesitated a moment. She had all these conflicting emotions amidst her drunkenness, which was still working itself through her body. This was either the dumbest thing she'd ever done, or it was one of the best things to happen to her in a while. She already felt like she was falling for him, but how was that possible? She could hear Lily clear as day in her head, as if she was sitting in the back seat with them. "Why are you doing this?" Lily kept asking her. But, the bride would not listen to her this time.

Stan was so charming, so easy to talk to. Smooth. Intelligent. Confident. Persuasive too–like she would believe, or pretend to believe, everything he said, even if it was a lie. But, she didn't even care if he was lying at this point. He worked in Sales and Marketing at work, and that seemed to fit his personality really well. And he was good at it. She began to feel really happy. Giddy even. A warm feeling, what could only be described as pure joy, came over her. Or so she interpreted it as such. Maybe it was the alcohol, but then maybe that had nothing to do with it. Regardless, she felt good. Really good.

"It's near Apollyon Boulevard, just past Belial Avenue. It's south of..."

Stan interrupted her.

"I know exactly where that is," he said. "Just sit back and relax. We'll be there in no time."

~

Joy didn't bloom right away in my life. There was always plenty of opportunity for me to fail. After all, I was raising three teenagers and at odds a great deal of the time with the Church. We don't always get to understand what's happening in our lives. Remembering that God was with me often took extra effort as well. Joy, though it is said to be the wellspring of life, didn't seem to be exuding through me. In fact, I think the world appeared to be much happier than me. I found myself in the middle of a strong learning curve that required a notable amount of discipline for my soul.

Putting seed in good rich soil produces the best tasting fruit, but it has to be incubated. When the tender shoot breaks forth, it must be protected. Strength begins to enrich the fruit once it begins to receive the kind of nourishment needed. I must have needed a lot of nourishment. My study time in the guide had increased. When I wasn't washing or ironing or cooking, I was studying. There was the occasional soccer game that I attended and indeed service to be done at the church as well, but my time in the greenhouse would prove to be that time I spent with love.

I am the vine; you are the branches. If a man remains in me and I in him he will bear much fruit. John 15:5

Jesus is telling us two distinct things here: that we are part of the same tree and that we also must "remain" in him. Just as Jesus is God and has that divinity in Him, so too we have access to that divine nature via the Holy Spirit when we accept Him as Savior. We can get in touch with that indwelling spirit that God breathed originally into Adam, that part of the same "tree" that Jesus is part of. At the same time, when we "remain" in Him (the Greek word is *meno*, which can also translate as "abide") and He in us, we will develop those spiritual fruits, such as joy, much like a tree that remains connected to its primary vine and root system, continuing to grow mightily and bear delicious fruit.

But, what exactly is joy? It's one of those words that sounds archaic, a word that people in this modern world don't have much use for. Most people understand the word "enjoy", which of course has the same origin, but not the same depth of meaning as simply "joy". Some would say it's a synonym for "happiness", but being happy doesn't quite cover it. According to many dictionary references, joy means cheerfulness, calm delight, gladness, and a feeling of great pleasure. However, those feelings, for the most part, are fleeting, temporary, or occasional. They have nothing to do with the overall or general state of "being happy" or contented, which is quite a different thing. True joy, the kind expressed in several passages in our guide, involves the quality of time–a permanent feeling, a foundational, long-lasting state of positive being, and an enduring or deep-rooted happiness or contentment. The world may claim to be contented and generally happy, but what is that true "joy" supposed to be found in, according to our guide?

If you have any encouragement from being united with Christ, if any comfort from his love, if any fellowship with his spirit, if any tenderness and compassion, then make my joy complete by being like minded, having the same love, being one in spirit and purpose. Philippians 2:2

Paul talks about the things that make his "joy complete"–having that "same love" and "being one in spirit and purpose". Ultimately, it's about being "united in Christ" and sharing in the love and eternal life that He brings anyone who follows Him. If I truly understood this, it didn't give me any room to be despondent. Of course, I could on any given day find some encouragement in Christ, and I knew that He loved me. I was fellowshipping with His spirit daily. But, I wasn't sure that I was experiencing what could be termed as "true joy". Being "like-minded" only seemed to happen when I was studying about these things in our guide, and not simply by trying to live my life through Christ.

Joy Blooms

I'm now on the staff of the church we had been attending for years. That in itself was a miracle since I didn't figure I could pay anyone to put me in any kind of position whatsoever. That's why I laughed the day I received a call from our Pastor who invited me to come on staff as the Director of Christian Education.

The Absence of Love

I asked him if he knew what he was doing, and he said, "Do you?"

The answer to that question would have been "No". However, the years of study with love had prepared me to present what I had learned to an audience of both adults and children. Our Sunday school department had better attendance with our adults than our children. I found that interesting since we had a very successful daycare in our church and had for more than fifteen years. There were plenty of children associated with the church, just not on Sunday.

The Pastor was less than enthusiastic about my desire to take the list of kids from the daycare to call their parents. I wanted to see if on Sunday morning we could pick their children up and bring them for an hour of Christian training. Pastor indicated to me that that had been tried before in other places he had served with little to no success. Still, I was granted permission and the Lord provided the way. Every Sunday, our church bus would fill up with children. In fact, we needed another bus. Then, there were two buses filled with children coming to learn about Jesus. Talk about joy! I was at least feeling it during that time!

Sunday School

Many of our Sunday school teachers were actually employed by the public school system. Here, it seemed, they had been taught not to speak or teach about Jesus. Without realizing it, this stream of thought had filtered right into Sunday school.

I now call the classes I conducted "Jesus 101". Every chance I got, I used his name. It kept things stirred up continually along with the fact that I personally had no continuing education in the eyes of those who had achieved documentation for higher education. My years at home at the foot of the cross with Jesus did not provide me with a certificate of completion. The fact is I wasn't "completed" but, rather, a work in progress. There may have been other reasons to go against my leadership, but joy was not turning out to be what I had hoped it would be in Him.

Though I had immense success in the bus ministry, there

were trials and tribulations and dissension. However, the opposition was not focused on me. It was the leader, our Pastor, who vehemently resisted. Joy seemed to be coming in short supply. Because I was a member of the staff, others wrongfully assumed I knew of plans that would divide our congregation. I didn't. There were many things we could have focused on to encourage our unity in Christ, but no one wanted to. That didn't seem so different in our home either.

Struggles with Our Daughter

Our daughter, Christy, was feisty and headstrong as a young adult. She was also a beautiful girl, and boys took to her, but sometimes not the kind of boy you'd want to take home to Mama. We struggled with the lifestyle she had chosen. She had fallen in love with her boyfriend, who was a professed unbeliever. Especially when we are young and naive, we sometimes get so wrapped up in our human feelings of love, sometimes a disguise for our animal lust, that we are blinded and lose sight of the bigger picture. Much as we would like to think that we can, in time, convert someone to whom we fall madly in love with, I believe our daughter was going against 2 Corinthians 6:13 in which Paul emphatically says "Do not be yoked together unequally with unbelievers". The phrase "yoked together unequally" is actually a translation of one Greek word, *heterozugeo*. The verb "to yoke" is to join together using a "yoke", which is a crossbar with two U-shaped pieces to enable two animals, such as oxen, to work together closely. Sometimes what feels like love or joy is our own base, animalistic desires posing as the real thing, drawing two people together who in the long run aren't compatible.

We had hoped that we could assist this young man in his own personal life because it had not been an easy one for him. The opposite happened, however, and the price we paid was supreme. It was an acute example of the reason that Paul talks against such "unequal yoking."

But, initially I felt I had done wrong in my approach and in the words I said to our daughter about the situation. I told God I would tell Christy I was sorry. I would go to her and let her know that I had not handled the circumstances properly. Before I decided to do that, though, I sat at His feet and listened for His voice. I couldn't believe what I heard.

I read in our guide in the book of First Samuel about Eli, the predecessor and master of Samuel, who had two sons. These sons were wicked boys. They would go to the "tent of the meeting place", sometimes called the tabernacle, which was the sacred tent used by the Israelites that contained the "most holy place" and housed the Ark of the Covenant, but not to pray or worship God–far from it. These bad boys would go there to select young women at random to have their way with them. It was clear that these boys did not know God, and never would. The Lord went to Eli about their behavior. He said, "If you do not restrain your sons from going to the tent of the meeting place and seducing these young girls, I will bring a curse upon you and your entire household". God promised Eli that his sons and daughters would die in the prime of life if he did not restrain them.

The Lord wasn't going to let me apologize, so I let my stinging words stand without apology. I know I was speaking truth, even if my approach was a little rough and biting. I knew the boy was bad news for our daughter, and I had said so. I prayed long and hard about the situation, but the message from the Lord to me was not to encourage her in this relationship, but also not to apologize to her for speaking the truth.

Within forty-eight hours, Christy was gone. She had decided it was time for her to return to her mother's. Our daughter had moved out of our home for good. It was that day that my husband's heart could barely breathe. Our lives were changed immensely, and we also learned a lot from this experience.

Challenges to Joy

There were many things that challenged my family and my joy in life, but what I have discovered is that sometimes it takes time for good fruit to be developed. Keeping my heart broken and contrite was a purpose that I hadn't wanted to sign up for. It left me feeling joyless at times. In this world, He says, you will have trouble, but fear not for I have overcome all. Yes, sometimes trouble is what we get, but the outcome is completely dependent upon faith. Did I keep my heart tender at church? Did I forgive when necessary? Did I continue to love our daughter? The answer to all was yes. But, did I run away from my problems? Sometimes I felt like I did, but I did not run away from love. In fact, I was more dependent than ever before. Faith was becoming part of my life blood.

I was slowly beginning to exchange my ways for His. It didn't mean that I was constantly happy. Sometimes my husband would ask me, "Where is the joy of the Lord in you, Sandy?" I admit I was often disappointed with myself, but I continued to press on towards the goal. Going back to what I had known as complete failure was not an option.

Paul, in the book of Philippians, says:

I always pray with joy because of your partnership in the gospel from the first day, being confident of this, that he who began a good work in you will carry it on to completion until the day of Christ Jesus. Phil. 1:4

What does it mean to "pray with joy"? It means the connection and communication that I make with the Lord every time I speak with Him has to contain that contentment I derive from being part of that same fruit-bearing tree, that same spirit, partnered with Him as a child of God. By making that commitment of faith, that's the first "good work". It continues as we live through Him, and on into the next life, ending with "the day of Christ Jesus", when He comes to reign on Earth at the end of time. That is the time in prophecy when the church as the Bride of Christ is fully united with her bridegroom, Jesus Himself.

What love was teaching me was that happiness evokes visions of a life without provocation. This means that my circumstances become dependent upon happiness. What if life wasn't going to turn out the way I thought it should? Would there never be any happiness?

Love was teaching me that joy is not dependent upon me. Joy was dependent upon Jesus Christ. He would be the one who defined my joy, just as He had been the one who had showed me His love. I was learning to trust Him even when life was uncertain and sometimes painful. My heart wasn't leading my life and my emotions could not either.

My joy was to be in my salvation (Psalm 51:12) and, though there were many tears, I would reap in joy (Psalm 126:5). The joy of the Lord is my strength and my faith was getting stronger every day.

Now I can say with fullness of heart, "The Lord is my strength and my shield; my heart trusts in him, and I am helped." (Psalm 28:7) I was entering into the joy of the Lord, to "share in my master's happiness." (Matthew 25:21)

You did not choose me but I chose you and appointed you to go and bear fruit—fruit that will last. John 15:16

Ultimately, my joy needs to derive from the fact that, although I can accept His love, He first chose me. Therefore, He loved me first!

Chapter Eight
Faith

Since we have been justified through faith, we have peace with God and our Lord Jesus Christ. Romans 5:1

As they pulled away from the house, the bride and Stan chatted for a couple minutes about unimportant things–this side of town, the weather, their work. She began feeling really good about herself. Maybe there was hope for her. After several failed relationships, and several more that never really got off the ground, here was a handsome, intelligent, caring man–at least he appeared to care about what she had to say–and she couldn't remember when was the last time that had happened to her.

Sure, she was drunk. Way drunk. But, she deserved a little fun once in a while, she reasoned. It was only wine and a few beers, after all–no hard liquor. It didn't take much to affect her, though. Anyway, he did the right thing to offer her a ride home, and she had enough wits about her to refuse, if she wanted to. But, she didn't want to. She enjoyed Stan's company. After all, it was her Jaguar, she thought, and it was a very safe car. What could possibly go wrong?

She could hear Lily now. The bride knew she would have to tell her. Even though she wasn't at the party, Lily knew many of the same people who did attend, so she was bound to find out that things got a little out of hand. After this night was done, she thought, she would tell Lily herself before she found out from others. The bride had tried to keep secrets from her before, but she would always find out. It was like Lily could read minds.

The bride decided she would tell her before she heard it from someone else. Maybe that would help her best friend to receive the news better. Lily was her confidante, her comfort, and her support–and she really appreciated her, relied on her, loved her. Still, the bride was sure Lily would let her have it and wouldn't hear the end of it. Lily was a real party-pooper sometimes.

Against her better judgment, she began opening doors in her conversation with Stan that she knew she shouldn't. But, she didn't care.

"So, do you have someone special in your life right now?" she asked.

"Special?" he asked with more than a hint of sarcasm in his voice. "As in, a significant other, a better half, a life partner…a goyle-friend?" He pronounced the word with that funny, mocking tone on purpose.

The bride immediately felt embarrassed having asked. She knew he was poking fun at the question. But, she still wanted to know. She felt she needed to know. Before she said anymore, he continued.

"Nah. I've dated here and there, but I don't have anyone I'm serious about."

She could tell he was lying. At least, she felt that he probably had a lot of "girlfriends" that he saw on a regular basis, as in the kind with benefits and no strings attached. Probably a lot of one night stands too. I don't think the word "faithful" was in his vocabulary. But she didn't let on that she felt this way. She began feeling competitive to all of those other women, silly as that was. Again, she felt hopeful about her own chances with him. But, she didn't want to be one of those many "girlfriends". She wanted a relationship. She tried to convince herself that maybe Stan just hadn't met the right girl. And, maybe she was that girl.

"Well, that's something we have in common, then," the bride responded.

"That's good,' he said. "By the way, we're almost at Belial Avenue. How much farther?"

"Turn left at Abyss. It's the next one after Belial. Then, it's just a few houses down on the left."

"Alright, then. Man, I can't believe how smoothly this car drives. Considering the amount of power it packs."

"Yeah, I know. It's quite a beauty, isn't it?"

"Sure is. And so are you."

~

With our daughter Christy at her mother's and Troy, our eldest, now in the military, our middle son, Todd, was graduating from high school and preparing to enlist in the military. That very same year, our youngest son, Chris, was beginning his education in kindergarten. What a range to raise, huh?

I'll never forget that October when little Christopher was experiencing his first Halloween celebration at Woodland Elementary in Zephyrhills, Florida. The same principal of the school was there when my first three children had been educated. He recognized me from those many years ago when my two older boys attended and I was there with them. With some surprise on his face, he said: "You are here just to help out, right?" I pointed out my youngest son, whose hair was a beautiful bright red, and said, "He is mine". This was met with the principal's response, "Your kind scares me to death!" Indeed!

Christopher had received the fullness of my faith since his conception. He was engulfed by my faith and the life that had become my own. Upon picking him up from school one afternoon I found him in tears. He had spoken to me for three months about wanting to be home-schooled. I had no idea what that would entail nor any intention of taking on that kind of responsibility. The public school system had educated every member of our family. Today, however, I listened.

It seemed during recess our youngest son had taken his

show-and-tell soccer ball to school. A more aggressive child had decided to take ownership of the ball at a time when all children were to return to the classroom. Trying to regain possession of his property prompted another student to attempt to help which, by now, had drawn attention to those in authority. The child demanding the return of said ball to our son was spotted at just that moment and trouble ensued. Because this unknown young child attempted to help our son, he got in trouble and this was where the plethora of tears was coming from while sharing his story with me. Needless to say, I agreed with Christopher's plea to homeschool him.

Meanwhile, Troy was at the line of demarcation in Korea, and Todd was jumping out of airplanes. Our daughter's life brought a beautiful new grandson into being. I had been parenting for nearly a quarter of a century and, honestly, I wasn't ready to be a grandparent. I had poured my heart into our four children and couldn't imagine loving anyone as much as my husband and I had loved our children. But love that little grandson we did, as much as our own children. Love knows no bounds!

What is Faith?

Faith. For those engrained in the spiritual, this third "fruit of the spirit" is a word we hear all the time in church and religious circles. In the secular world, this word is usually used in the longer adjective and adverb versions, faithful or faithfully, rather than the simple noun. Good words, but they somehow lose the luster of plain ol' faith, mostly because they are so overused as to become watered down from their original meaning. Still, we hear the noun in half-hearted clichés like "keep the faith" or taking that "leap of faith", though I would agree, especially early in life, it was a "leap" for me. And, for many, "keeping the faith" is a struggle.

Some would say "belief" and "faith" are the same thing. Indeed, the words are often used to define each other. A study of the Greek would seem to bear that out. The Greek words for the noun faith and the verb believe (*pistis* and *pistevo*–literally, to have faith) are similar and share the same root. But, where does that leave us in understanding these words?

The meaning of both words connotes trust, persuasion, perseverance, confidence, or reliance on a single idea, person, or thing. Faith also has the connotation of commitment, as well as steadfast hope, enduring belief, unshakeable truth, and permanent trust. To "put your faith in something" is a stronger phrase than simply "believing" in it. The English-speaking world seems to have replaced the word faith with belief. To my modern ears, faith has a stronger, spiritual quality, while the word "belief" (as in Big Foot or UFOs being put on the same footing as a supreme being) seems a weaker word with its ubiquity. We don't put our "faith" in the Loch Ness monster, but certainly many of us do in our Lord and Savior Jesus Christ.

It's similar to the difference between happiness and joy–the elements of strength and time (foundational and eternal) seem clearer with faith than simply "believing" in something. We need more than "something to believe in". We need to define what that "something" is. Faith seems to be specific; belief tends to be vague. We can't afford to be vague when souls are at stake.

Pilgrimage of Faith

I definitely took that "leap of faith" in venturing into home schooling with my youngest. Home schooling was not well accepted by the public education system. Still, I complied with every requirement the state of Florida had encumbered the home schooled child with. It was a struggle at times, both for me and for Christopher, but it ended up being a blessing from God that day he pleaded with me to take up the formal education of him at home.

With trust in God, our family of three traveled to England to live and work. Our son's English Literature book had on its cover soldiers at Buckingham Palace, the mysteriously placed rocks of Stonehenge, and the Eiffel Tower, all of which we traveled to. Our hands-on education was alive with interest as I traveled with our son through England, Belgium, and France. We crossed the English Channel as often as we got the opportunity to do so.

I was speaking at the Full Gospel Businessmen's Association in England and in the prison at Maidstone. Our family was attending church at Bearsted Methodist where I was able to share my faith at the local women's group. Our home was opened to gatherings for others who too were on this pilgrimage of faith. The welcome we received in this church was filled with the "healing balm of Gilead" referenced in Jeremiah 8. There were many words of knowledge, healing, and prophecy during our time there. My heart soared when the Lord gave me clear instructions in the life that was lived in my cherished and now-departed friend Molly. She was a dear friend and will not be forgotten in this world.

So what was this faith being built up in me composed of? The book of Acts begins by telling me in the following manner.

Confirming the souls of the disciples and exhorting them to continue in the faith and that we must through much tribulation enter into the kingdom of God. Acts 14:22

Great faith accomplishes many things, as written about in our guide. Our hearts are purified (Acts 15:9). We are sanctified (Act 26:18). Obedience to faith (Romans 16:26) is involved, as well as righteousness (Romans 4:13). Faith comes by hearing and hearing by the word of God (Romans 10:17). I was listening on a regular basis.

Trials

Learning not to think too highly of myself is an ongoing process according to the measure of faith God has given me (Romans 12:3). I'm still intimidated sometimes by the knowledge of man, but knowing that I should stand in the power of God (I Corinthians 2:5), it still remains a cry of my heart to date. I do continue to stand fast in the faith (I Corinthians 16:13) as I learn to walk by faith, not by sight (II Corinthians 5:7) as often as possible.

The spirit seems to be the part of me that responds properly to the perfecting of my faith. This is where the promise of the Spirit through faith accomplishes in me what in my own strength and power I am unable to do. Remember that God's love covenant said that if I decided to love Him that he would be faithful and merciful to me. Faith working by love (Galatians 5:6) exposes me to the "refiner's fire." (Zechariah 13:9) The metaphor of purifying or "refining" precious metals with heat is used in several places in the Bible to represent spiritual purification. Many times, this purification was something that most would not sign up for. I certainly resisted it.

James talks about faith this way:

Consider it pure joy, my brothers, whenever you face trials of many kinds because you know that the testing of your faith develops perseverance. Perseverance must finish its work so that you may be mature and complete, not lacking anything. James 1:2

Not resenting trouble when it comes is a response that He continues to work in me. Intellectual agreement attempts to pass for true faith sometimes. It is easy to say we have faith, but true faith produces loving actions toward others–a commodity in short supply in my world, and maybe in your world too.

Steadfastness

Have you noticed that, in a world of dysfunctional families, and mine would definitely be considered by most to qualify, how difficult it is to respond with loving actions?

I was determined to continue to grow in my faith. Steadfastness is becoming a lifestyle that has taken more than thirty years to develop and stabilize. I've discovered that one must contend for the faith. I'm to "fight the good fight of faith" (I Timothy 6:12), speak words of faith and rebuke sharply in faith (Titus 1:13).

Still, faith seems to be a difficult concept to wrap our heads around. There is a part of faith that is a gift from God, but, as it says in Romans 12:3, "every man has been given a measure (or portion) of faith." We all have been given it, to some degree. So, why is faith so difficult to discuss?

My research tells me that faith alone contributes so much to our lives. Knowing that it is impossible to please God without faith (Hebrews 11:6) makes having it all the more necessary to my love story. Faith is the substance of things hoped for, and the evidence of things not seen (Hebrews 11:1). Faith can also seem a bit elusive or even illusory. Sometimes it just doesn't "feel" real. Faith must be accomplished before the evidence (or even when no physical evidence) often springs forth of its presence.

Not so long ago, I heard the Lord speak to me about my faith. He said my faith is nearly complete in one area of my life–my finances! Who would ever conceive that faith and finances had any kind of relationship at all? Believing by faith provides the essence of substance that will sure enough burst forth out of us when He is in it. Holding the course by faith until it is brought into completion is a life that will demonstrate patience (another "fruit of the spirit") and will respond in love. It is no wonder, then, that love, the motivation to write this book, is so woven into our substance contributed by faith.

Today, I contend for the faith while building myself up through studying the word contained throughout our guide. A passion has developed in me for it. It is now in my heart that through love we can be united and share in the joy that comes from true, steadfast faith.

His Testimony

Throughout this book, I have been sharing my testimony of how God's love changed my life. It is here that I want to share God's testimony of His love for us. After all, this is truly about His love dedicated to our eternal well-being that He by His spirit births in us, then keeps us through faith in Him and brings us into maturity–a bride without spot or blemish. It is His love story.

We accept man's testimony, but God's testimony is greater because it is the testimony of God, which he has given about his Son. Anyone who believes in the Son of God has this testimony in his heart. Anyone who does not believe God has made him out to be a liar, because he has not believed the testimony God has given about his Son. And this is the testimony: God has given us eternal life, and this life is in his Son. He who has the Son has life; he who does not have the Son of God does not have life. I John 5:9-12

How can you say it more simply than that? "He who has the Son has life". While struggling through life with the bumps and bruises dealt each one of us, again I heard Him speak to my heart. "Sandy, every day you get up and leave the house with a picnic basket in your hand while I am at war." You see, I was complaining about some scar I had received, perhaps invisible, but just as painful as the black-and-blue type. I just couldn't understand why I would get these "scars" and suffer such painful trials at times. I was engaged in reading the Word, serving, and praying. Why did He not protect me? Ever had such a thought?

In this world, we will all have trouble. Becoming a Christian does not keep that from happening. I also found out that, no matter how long we serve by faith, in this world we will never "arrive". Honestly, I thought it would be different. It was really quite a revelation to find out that even with the fruits of the spirit developing and operating in my life, I would never in this world be free of sin. I think all Christians should wear a sign that says, "Under construction". Somewhere, somebody decided that Christians think they are perfect. Does anyone know where that came from?

If you consider yourself a Christian, you've probably heard this before: "And you call yourself a Christian!" Or maybe you've felt disappointed in yourself because, by faith, you know to live differently, but your actions sum up your need for something greater than yourself, or at least what you've become so far. Sometimes I'm certain I am my own worst enemy.

The Absence of Love

Then one day I was reading from our guide and I noticed what is the shortest scripture in the King James translation. It's John 11:35, and it says simply "Jesus wept". In another scripture, it says He was acquainted with grief and then pleaded with Jerusalem that "if only you knew what would bring you your peace" (Luke 19:42). I received a revelation that made dealing with my own troubles a bit less difficult. If Jesus could not reason with man or gain their understanding, and if He had pain to the degree that he wept, then perhaps my failures were not that at all. Maybe the outcome of faith wasn't what I saw today, but what I believed He said about tomorrow.

As it says in Revelation, He is the Alpha and the Omega, the beginning and the end. It didn't make going through a difficult place in my life easier, but it did put it into perspective. That's exactly what faith is in the process of developing in me. His perspective! It would take time and I had not forgotten that my way simply did not work. I would press on toward the goal, to be that beautiful bride for Christ Jesus who, with the Holy Spirit working in me, is my hope of glory. Despite my human limitations, He loved me anyway!

Chapter Nine
Patience

Faith and patience inherit the promises. Hebrews 6:12

The drive to her home took only about 10 minutes, but it seemed longer. Her mind was swimming in emotion at this point, but maybe that was the alcohol too. Stan certainly gave her a lot to think about. The bride was not used to being given the kind of compliments that he was lavishing on her, like calling her a beauty and all. She was many things, but she didn't feel that was a word that described her, especially on a first date. "There I go again" she thought, overanalyzing what was going on. A simple drive home from a party by a nice guy like Stan wasn't a date. It wasn't that she didn't enjoy the kind words, though. She loved the attention, even if there were half-truths attached to it.

"Which house is it?" Stan asked her as he turned onto Abyss Street, passing a Dead End sign at the edge of the road. The street was very pretty, lined with evenly-placed street lamps a couple houses apart. Several of the houses had oak trees in the modest-sized front lawns, helping to dim the full moon in the starry night sky.

"The last house on the left, at the end of the cul-de-sac," she answered. The street lamp they just passed was out, casting the left side of the dead end in darkness. The bride was relieved she had a man like Stan to see her in.

"I love these kinds of streets," he said. "Less neighbors to

The Absence of Love

worry about."

"Yeah, that's true. Mine are pretty cool. Seems like they're not home most of the time...oh, it's this one here." She pointed to an elegant Mediterranean-style home sitting at the dead end on the left side. It had lightly-colored stone walls, an arched entranceway, and a red, ceramic tile roof. "You can just pull up in the driveway."

Stan pulled the Jaguar up the incline, admiring the house as he did. The outside light was off, but there were some dim, solar-powered edge lights lining the walk way to the pretty arch leading to the red front door. The yard was kept up nicely, but he guessed that she didn't maintain it–and he was right. She paid a lawn service handsomely for the upkeep and it showed. The St Augustine grass was nicely mowed and weed-free, with three levels of shrubs and flowering plants along the front.

"I'll call for a taxi from here, " he said. "Shouldn't take long."

Stan put the car into park, got out quickly, and hopped around to help her out of the passenger side. She definitely needed the help. He opened the door for her and let her try to get out herself, but she had a hard time moving. The alcohol was still heavy in her bloodstream. He put his hand out. She hesitated taking it. She looked up at him, and finally put her hand in his. He pulled her up as she got out of the car and wobbled to her feet.

"Wow," she said. "I guess I'm worse off than I thought." She stood for a few seconds, making sure she had her balance, before taking her first step.

"That's okay," he said reassuringly. "I know the feeling. I'm going to call the taxi service I know. Used them before."

"Okay," she said, as he got out his cell phone and started dialing. She suddenly felt awkward about this whole situation. Was she just going to say goodbye to him and go into her house, leaving him standing out here in the dark while he waited for the taxi to pick him up? He didn't seem to mind, as he started walking down the driveway a bit toward the street, talking to the taxi service. When he put his cell away, he turned and looked at her up the driveway.

Despite her drunkenness, she would have looked attractive

even to someone completely sober. She wore a short-sleeved black dress that came up just above her knees, showing off her nice legs. She had on black sandals, as well as silver earring hoops and a matching plain silver bracelet. Nothing spectacular, but she had a decent body that wore this ensemble well. She had natural good looks that didn't require much make-up. With her brownish hair hinting of auburn, her big, brown eyes, and smooth, tan skin, she would have been regarded as pretty sexy by most standards.

"Um..." she said, against her better judgment. "You want to come in while you wait for the taxi? It's a little chilly out here." It was an unexpected 50 degrees–cool for August.

"No, that's okay. I'll just wait out here," he said as he put his hands in his pockets. "It should only be about a half-hour or so."

At that comment, she felt guilty. Here was a nice guy who made an effort to offer her a nice, safe, pleasant ride home. How could she leave him out in the cold? She didn't want to force him to come inside, but it seemed silly to have him wait in her driveway for the taxi.

"Well, you can come in if you want. I'll be up for a little bit to try to wind down before calling it a night." She wasn't sure why she said that. She wasn't even sure what that meant either.

"That's okay–I'll stay out here."

Now she was actually feeling herself get impatient with him. She wanted him to come inside–she didn't really understand why, and still wasn't thinking clearly. But, her confidence got the best of her.

"Listen, Stan. It's cold out here. Just come in and sit for a minute. I could even make some coffee for you–de-caf is what I'm having."

He waited a beat, and then smiled at her as he started walking back up the driveway toward her.

"Okay, sure. If you insist. I can't turn that down."

"Good."

At that, she turned around and walked with a bit of a stagger into her entranceway. She fumbled in her purse for her keys for a moment, finally finding them. Clumsily, she stuck the right key in the deadbolt lock of the front door, turned the handle, and opened the front door. It made an eerie creaking sound as it opened, like one you'd hear in an old horror movie.

"Wow, sounds like something needs WD-40", Stan said, as she walked through the door entrance.

"Yeah, I've been meaning to," she responded. "I have an alarm system, but I never turn it on. It's my alarm substitute, I guess. You can hear it all through the house."

"I'm sure you're right," he agreed.

She stepped in the foyer, with Stan right behind her. She flipped on the light, and closed the front door. The light blinded both of them for a moment, as their eyes had to get readjusted after having stood outside in the dark for several minutes.

"If you need to use the restroom, the guest bath is on your right there." She pointed down a hallway to the left of the foyer. "I'll go and make the coffee." She walked into the kitchen and began getting out the de-caf to make a small pot.

"I think I'll do that," Stan said, as he strolled down the hallway to the bathroom on the right. He closed the door behind him.

The bride thought for a moment–how did all of this just happen? It's late at night and, when she should be in bed asleep, she has invited a man into her house, and now she is making him coffee. The irrepressible Lily would be screaming at her right about now when she finds out about this. "Are you crazy!?" she could hear her yelling at her. "What were you thinking!?" Well, maybe she *was* crazy at this moment, and she was thinking that she hadn't had a good man–a real gentleman–over to her house in a while. Sure, he was about to leave, but at least they have developed this friendship to a place where maybe it could go somewhere in the future. She would make sure to ask for his cell phone number before he left.

She heard the toilet flush and then the sink water running, so she got the cups and saucers out to have the coffee poured when ready. Stan walked into the kitchen just as she turned around.

"Wow, you got a nice home here. I'm not surprised, considering the car you drive. They fit together perfectly."

She blushed and didn't know what to say for a moment, so he continued.

"Hey, could you show me around? I was thinking of doing some remodeling myself, and need some ideas. I get my kids sometimes on weekends and I need to do something about the space I have. I love the open spaces you have here."

That was news to her. Apparently divorced. She didn't want to pry, so she didn't ask any questions.

"Sure," she said as she motioned for him to follow her. "It's a split great-room plan." She indicated with an open hand the large living room in the front. There's two bedrooms on one side..."

"And a master bedroom and bath on the other?" he interrupted her.

"That's right," she said. "Here, follow me down this hallway." They walked toward the master bedroom side of the house.

Stan walked behind her, admiring what he saw–which had nothing to do with the house.

~

Deciding to love God predestines faith to produce our guide's promises in me. This takes time in most people–it did in me. It was inevitable that patience would have to be developed. This would also take a lot of love.

I don't know about your disposition, but I know mine is not inclined to patience. By definition, it infers long suffering; in fact many have chosen to use this translation rather than patience in the scriptures when addressing this "fruit of the spirit". The word patience is translated from two different Greek words throughout scripture: *makrothumia* and *hupomone*.

The first word, *makrothumia*, is a combination of two words: *macros*, meaning "long", and *thumos*, meaning "temper". This word implies the factor of time, and the ability to endure persecution and ill-treatment without having an out-of-control "temper" (as in a "bad" one) that results in restraint, rather than revenge or other negative behavior.

The second word, *hupomone*, is translated literally as "endurance". It implies such ideas as constancy, perseverance, bearing up (forbearance), steadfastness, and holding out. The word combines *hupo*, meaning "under," and *mone*, "to remain." It describes the capacity to continue to hold up under difficult circumstances, not with a passive complacency, but with a hopeful strength that resists defeat.

Regardless of the usage, this long-suffering contributes something to the soul that seems very unnatural. Who enjoys suffering? Certainly I didn't. If Love was going to accomplish its way in me, I was going to have to submit to challenges that would implement patience.

Skin Condition

At about age 10, I remember walking up a blacktopped walkway to the local high school in Cornell, Illinois. I don't remember why we were going there, but I was with my sister and mother. I don't think I was keeping pace because I have a vague memory of my mother's distress with me. Trying desperately to keep up, I fell. There was pain and a bit of bleeding–nothing overly serious. However, the injury never healed up properly. Mother took me to the doctor's. The red scaly patches of skin that covered the injured area had not healed properly. I was diagnosed with wool allergies, despite the fact that this skin condition was spreading throughout my extremities, even when I wasn't wearing any wool. I received an injection every day for approximately one year before going to a specialist who promptly diagnosed me with psoriasis.

Psoriasis is an incurable skin disease that, depending on which dispensation of medical advice we sought, had different recommended treatments. There was Librium prescribed for a season, and then arsenic. Twenty-one drops a day I took of this poison which today is no longer used as treatment. This all took place before high school. By then, I was using a coal tar ointment daily with coal tar baths. I remember telling my mother I would not get into that "black water" and she said fine, I could just keep the psoriasis. Then, it was a disease of the nervous system; now, it seems it is an immune system deficiency. In any event, this disease is considered genetic. My father ended up having this disease, but for much of his life it had laid dormant in him. It wasn't until I was diagnosed with psoriasis that he even knew he had it.

My parents didn't have the kind of money needed to treat my skin disease, so Grandma and Grandpa picked up the costs for all my medicine. As I reflect on it today years after they have gone to be with Jesus, I realize the extent of their gift as an unselfish act of their love for me. At the time, I was just a kid and didn't understand.

While swimming at a local pool one summer, I was asked by the owners to leave. It seems my skin was causing a problem for others swimmers at the time. Though psoriasis is not contagious, it certainly looks like it could be.

I also remember a time when I was walking down the halls at high school on a rare day when I decided to wear panty hose. Behind me, I heard a couple young men laughing and talking a bit loud. They were talking about the number of runs I had in my nylons. They weren't runs–it was my psoriasis showing through. Most days found me either wearing knee socks or pants to cover my disgrace.

A Different Way to Live

There was an advertisement on television that talks about the heartbreak of psoriasis. Perhaps even that would have been bearable; however, it didn't stop there. When bombarded with poor self-image, the mind resorts to many things to soothe the pain. Looking for love was now a full time occupation for me.

When I attended Weaver Airline School, my goal was to become a stewardess. However, I was too young, not to mention I dealt with psoriasis a great deal of the time. Still, travel was possible as a reservationist, so that was the job I took with American Airlines afer they hired me from the Airline School.

Unknown to me at this time in my life, there was a different way to live than the one I had chosen. To find the illusive love of my life, I would have to make some changes, but didn't know what those were yet. This lack of knowledge, coupled with my own sinful desires, bad decisions, and the pain I felt, both physical and emotional, were just the recipe needed for a strong dose of patience to develop in me. Like an airplane flying through a storm, the next ten years of my life would be especially turbulent.

Another Word for Patience

An old English word that is sometimes used in place of patience is a word that's fun to throw out at a dinner party when you want to sound smart–longanimity. Defined as "disposition to bear injuries patiently" this quality is one I needed desperately. It's from the Latin words *longus animus* ("long soul"). Again, the factor of time is brought in, as well as the spiritual concept of the soul. Psoriasis has no known cure, so having to deal with this battle longanimitously caused my soul to suffer greatly. Additionally, I longed for a cure, but one did not come, despite pleading with God over and over again. It would continue to plague me for years to come.

So, how exactly does God factor into my skin disease? This question is related to the number one question about God many people, including my Grandpa, struggle with–believers and non-believers alike–namely, why does a loving God allow "bad" things to happen to "good" people? Specifically for me, the question was: How could love endure such embarrassment? Why after years of obedience, study, and faith–and good old-fashioned praying to God to take this burden from me–do I still deal with psoriasis? Trust me, there is no emotion nor question that I have not asked. This much I know: regardless of the impact psoriasis has had in my life, I was not going to give up on love. I was committed to this relationship, just as a bride and groom commit to each other, in good times and in bad, in sickness and in health.

Here is some of what I know which will accentuate what I don't know about patience or long suffering. In addition to longanimity, it means forbearance, fortitude, and endurance. You need to be in it for the long haul, no matter the circumstances. So, the fact that I didn't want this challenge in my life was irrelevant. I learned that what I want and what God gives me or simply allows to happen are different things. Patience is a fruit of the spirit that was planted as a seed and eventually would grow, but it was going to take love's endurance in me to make that happen.

Do you show contempt for the riches of His kindness, tolerance and patience, not realizing that God's kindness leads you toward repentance? Romans 2:4

Honestly, I have shown contempt for His tolerance of this disease. Thank God His kindness does lead towards repentance, which I would learn about later in life. Thinking about it now, blaming God for my problem was ridiculous since most would consider Him to be the closest thing to perfect that there is. Yet my sinful nature needed to blame, in its weakness, and it did. There was a battle raging inside me. I fought my own belief at times, and some days wasn't sure if I could continue to believe in that concept of true love–that agape love in all of its forms. It seemed too far for me to reach. I felt disconnected at times from God–empty and incomplete. Some of it was my own self-pity that I wallowed in. My problems outweighed my ability to grow with patience.

What if God, choosing to show his wrath and make his power known, bore with great patience the objects of his wrath—prepared for destruction? What if he did this to make the riches of his glory known to the objects of his mercy, whom He prepared in advance for glory – even us...Romans 9:22-24

I don't think God likes it when evil gets away with anything. To a certain extent, that is what psoriasis is. He has chosen a time and bears with great patience for us to come into the riches of His glory. I must pursue love by faith and not forget that it is His kindness, tolerance, and patience that will attain the riches of His glory for me.

...being strengthened with all power according to His glorious might so that you may have a great endurance and patience and joyfully give thanks to the Father, who has qualified you to share in His inheritance. Colossians 1:11

We can't give up! When I'm uncomfortable, when life doesn't go the way it would be pleasing to my soul, we will only be strengthened if we endure. Through doing what our guide instructs, we gain experience and staying power. With love, we can survive–we can make it! Stamina will be produced when that fruit of the spirit, patience, continues to mature in us. Is it possible we can believe this? Is it possible I could? Even when I wasn't there, even when I had no patience left, it seemed, I still had hope. But, would that hope ultimately disappoint me? Paul talks about the result of these fruits in him, as well as his trials, in second Timothy:

You know all about my way of life, my purpose, faith, patience, love, endurance, persecutions, sufferings–the Lord rescued me from them all. II Tim 3:10

Would He rescue me from my suffering? Was God waiting patiently for me? (I Peter 3:2) What were the challenges love would require of me while producing this long-suffering fruit of the spirit? Did I even have enough patience for patience? Sometimes I wasn't sure if I was even interested in those answers. Listen!

..as servants of God we commend ourselves in every way: in great endurance; in troubles, hardships and distresses; in beatings, imprisonments and riots; in hard work, sleepless nights and hunger; in purity, understanding, patience and kindness; in the

Holy Spirit and in sincere love; in truthful speech and in the power of God. II Corinthians 6:3-7

Since we have long determined that God is love, then we too must commend ourselves in every way to Him. Had I?

If we know so much, then why is it necessary to question God? My reasoning mind would have to answer this and many other questions. This I now believed: No matter what my responses to it, love would not forsake me. Would I give up on love when the going got tough?

When you look in a mirror and detest what you see (a body covered in psoriasis), would I run away and hide or would I stand with love? When someone you love separates from another that you love, would my heart harden? When those I supported over the years have an opportunity to do the same to me and don't, would I become bitter? When the man you love decides to love someone else, would love be victorious in me? When my husband decides to go to work in Iraq and Saudi Arabia, would I run or stay the course? When God asks me into service and others can't see the call on my life, would I believe love? Oh!–what challenges there were and would continue to be in my life that would bring me to the core of what being patient was all about. Apart from God, I soon learned, I could do nothing!

How could I have the kind of patience it took to be prepared, preach the word, and offer correction and encouragement as I felt led to do–for my husband, my children, my friends, and anyone who I came in contact with–if living my life brought bitterness and hatred into my heart? I couldn't!

Love takes the circumstances of our lives–under the tutelage of our guide with our commitment to love–and begins to teach each one who is willing how to overcome in this world. Would I stay the course?

Christ Jesus displayed His unlimited patience as an example for those who would believe and receive eternal life. I Timothy 1:16

Would I?

Chapter Ten
Temperance

Knowing this, that our old man is crucified with him, that the body of sin might be destroyed, that henceforth we should not serve sin.
Romans 6:6

The bride entered her bedroom, with Stan following closely behind. The bed was a king-size four-poster adorned with an elegant quilt, a few comfy pillows, and pretty ruffles along the edge–it was like a princess's bed, with the only thing missing an ornate canopy on top. The room was sparsely furnished, with an old-fashioned dresser drawers that matched the bed and a make-up table and mirror in the corner.

"The bed is nothing special," she told him, "but what I love is my closet. Are your kids girls?"

"Kids?" he asked.

"Yeah. Do you have girls or boys?"

"Oh, two girls." Her back was still towards him, and he liked her from that angle. He moved closer to her as she walked into an enormous closet, with racks and hangers galore, and several cubby holes and other organizers to neatly arrange a plethora of clothing items and accessories. Some of the drawers had a lock on them–apparently those were off-limits. It was hard to believe the items in this small room were just for one person. The closet was decked out with a wide array of dresses, skirts, blouses, T-shirts, shorts, pants, and dozens of shoes–from flip-flops to high-heels.

"How old are they?" She turned around as she said this. She indeed was pretty. She looked up at him and blinked. Her big, brown eyes had eyeliner that made them pop, with subtle eye shadow and long, thick eyelashes. "Come hither, Stan" she seemed to say.

"Oh, they're...old enough. Younger than they'd like to be, and older than they look." He was the father of lies, exceptionally good at making up convincing stuff on the spot–and selling it without batting an eye. He hesitated a moment, and looked away from the bride with feigned sadness, then continued.

"Can we not talk about them right now?"

"I'm sorry," she offered as apology. "Sore subject, I'm sure, if your ex has custody."

"Yeah, she does," he managed, turning his head back and staring straight into those eyes. She immediately felt sympathy for him. He kept staring at her, and those eyes burrowed into hers. She felt her soul being pulled toward him, in a way she had never experienced before. She suddenly felt a wave of anticipatory pleasure come over her. She wanted him. She knew that was wrong, but the guilt was outweighed by the chance at euphoria that could result.

"Um... your taxi is probably almost here, so...is there anything else I could show you?" She just stepped into that one.

"Yeah, lots," he said as he reached his hand out to touch the side of her face. "You know you are a beautiful girl."

"I...I don't know you," she stammered, as he leaned in closer to her.

"Well, let's fix that," as his lips forced themselves against hers. She allowed it for a few seconds, but then backed away. He pressed in again, pushing her against some leather coats on a closet wall. She started to give in to her desires, knowing there was a battle raging in her. She wanted to remain in control, but was losing the fight. She was still very drunk, and wasn't able to defend herself. He was an aggressive kisser, and she liked men who could take control like that, when she was a willing participant. She felt her body doing things that her mind was not giving approval for, but she didn't have the strength to push him away. She wrapped her arms around him, and she heard him moan as he continued to kiss her, moving down to her cheek and neck. Then, she thought she heard a noise.

"I think I hear the door bell," she said, hoping.

"You couldn't have. There's no taxi," he said, as he put his arms firmly around her, pushing her deeper into the closet, knocking some skirts and blouses off their hangers.

"What?" she said, as she tried to wriggle free, while at the same time struggling with the urge to simply give in to him.

"I didn't call a taxi," he said matter-of-factly.

"Why...." He had a strong grip on her by now. She resisted the urge to scream. No one would hear her anyway.

"I just figured you'd tell me I could spend the night here. I know that's what you and I both want," he said confidently, as he moved in again. This time, she pushed him back.

"No, it's not," she said sharply, with some attitude.

"Come on, you know you want it."

One side of her knew that was true. Her animal lust was telling her to give in, but she had begun sobering up just enough to realize she had made a big mistake letting him in her house. She tried pushing away from him, but he was a strong man.

"Let go of me," she pleaded softly.

"Alright, okay...I will," he said. He let go of his grip on her, and backed up out of the closet. He was still facing her, but he allowed her enough space to get out of the closet door. She glanced toward the bedroom door, and their eyes met again. She bolted for it. He blocked her path. He closed and locked the handle on the bedroom door.

"Oh, you're not going to get away that easy," he said.

"This is my house! Get out!" she screamed, holding out her right arm, pointing wildly toward the door. He ignored the gesture, and instead started moving toward her.

"Come on, baby. I just wanted to have a little fun..."

"You need to leave," she said, sternly but unconvincingly. She tried getting around him, but he grabbed her by the arms.

"I'm not going anywhere yet."

At that, he barreled forward with her in his grip, pushing

her onto the bed. She let out a gasp, and he grunted as he got on top of her. He straddled her, with his legs pinning her around her waist toward the head of the bed. He pushed her up against the decorative pillows laying at the headboard.

"Not until I get what I came for," he said. He began struggling to pull up her black dress. She started hitting his body and his face with her fists.

"No! I don't...No!" she screamed as she struggled with him, trying to flip him off her and turning toward her right side. He pushed her back down, grabbed the top of her dress, and ripped it straight down several inches, exposing more of her than she would have allowed if she were sober. Then, they both heard a sound. It was the same sound she thought she heard earlier. It was a clear, low, ringing sound. The door bell! This was followed by a loud, rapid knock on the door. It was well after midnight, so she had no idea who this could be. Stan obviously had no interest in finding out. He immediately pushed all his weight against her, grabbing both her arms and violently pushing them down onto her face to cover her mouth. He pushed down even harder and lower toward her throat, partially choking her. He was able to continue this pressure with one arm, his right, and he stretched out his body and lower limbs to keep her flailing legs from loosening his hold on her. With his free left hand, he reached down to begin pulling up her dress and pulling down what was underneath it. She had no more fight in her. She was past the point of resisting. He then moved that hand to his belt, unhinging it, and grabbed his fly with his thumb and forefinger, unzipping that. The weight of him on her was intense, and she was nearing exhaustion. She felt herself starting to black out, though she continued to struggle, weak as she was.

"Don't fight me. You're mine already."

Then, they both heard another noise. It was the front door slowly creaking open.

~

A commitment to love and to live by the spirit was the direction I wanted for my life. However, if we are honest with ourselves, most of us know about our own sinful nature. We don't like that part of us, even hate it, but still we have given way to sin.

Temperance is the older King James English word for the more modern concept of "self control". As late as the 19th and early 20th centuries, the word "temperance" was still a popular word, but its meaning was funneled down to abstaining from, or at least limiting the consumption of, alcoholic beverages. Various "temperance movements" and organizations, such as the American Temperance Society, gave rise eventually to the 18th amendment and the Prohibition Era in America, which itself prompted the repeal shortly thereafter with the 21st amendment. The point our country realized was, it wasn't the alcohol itself that was the problem or the removal of this freedom that solved it. The real issue was people's lack of self-control, which can be difficult to legislate in a free society. Scripture itself doesn't seem to be anti-alcohol (it can be argued that even Jesus himself drank fermented wine, just not to excess), but the over-indulgence in such things is where the line of "sin" is crossed. But, temperance means a lot more than simply abstinence from alcohol.

Although many words are used to describe temperance, such as moderation, sacrifice, forbearance, prudence, and restraint, one that stands out in my mind is "strength" which probably wouldn't even be found in my personal definition. In recent psychological texts, temperance is listed as a "character strength." Who knew self-control incorporated strength? No wonder I was so weak! Just as all the powers and abilities bestowed by God upon man, this one is capable of abuse. The right use of self-control demands the controlling power of the will under the operation of the Spirit of God. Righteousness represents God's claim, while self control is man's response.

Temperance is a "virtue" as well as a "fruit of the spirit" that masters one's desires and passions–including our propensity to addiction and over-indulgence in various pleasures at the expense of others or where it consumes our thoughts, particularly the sexual variety. Also, a lack of control of emotions, such as anger, border on sinful activity when not kept in check. Again, anger itself is not a sin, but, as Proverbs 14:9 says, those who are "slow to anger" have "great understanding". Many think of this as a unique problem for men, but women are not immune to a lack of self-control in many areas. I knew that to be true for me.

Ruler of this World

Up to this point, I haven't dealt much with the spiritual dimension of the title of the book. What does it mean to have an "absence of love"? A pure "love absence" or total removal of love would represent the antithesis of God–one such being that could represent this concept is Satan himself. Satan (or "the devil" as he is also called in our guide) is mentioned over 100 times in scripture. Using the King James translation as an example, Satan is referenced 49 times and "the devil" is referenced 56 times, with other references throughout, including the Old and New Testament. For those churches that have stopped preaching about Satan, I wonder which book they are using to derive their statement of faith.

We have certainly watered Satan down in our art, our culture, and even in our churches, but our guide clearly describes him as a real entity that has influence over this world. He is described as an "angel of light" (and called Lucifer or "light bearer" in Isaiah 14:12). He is the great fallen angel who, because of envy, was banished from heaven, along with his legion of followers (demons). He never specifically claimed he had more power than God (he always knew his place), only that he felt God wasn't essential and that he could rule better than Him.

When man and woman were created, they were given dominion over the earth, but that was before sin entered the world. There is strong evidence that, since that time, Satan himself has become the ruler of this world and the whole earth fell under his dominion. In 2 Corinthians 4:5, he is described as the "god of this age". In John 14:30, he is the "prince of this world." As John writes in his first epistle, "the whole world is under the control of the evil one" (1 John 5:19). Even Jesus, while being tempted by him in the desert, did not argue with Satan when he stated that the world belonged to him.

The devil led him up to a high place and showed him in an instant all the kingdoms of the world. And he said to him, "I will give you all their authority and splendor, for it has been given to me, and I can give it to anyone I want to. So if you worship me, it will all be yours. Luke 4:5-7

Of course, Satan is also called many other things in scripture–deceiver, liar, tempter, destroyer, murderer, the enemy, and many others. We must never forget that, lest we fall under his trap. It's unclear all the powers that Satan has, but evidence of other fallen angels (his demons) are throughout scripture, and are at work in the world. There is evidence that he can speak through dreams, as other angels can, and through the words and actions of other people. The world of the supernatural is mostly unknown to us, and we must be careful not to assign our human limitations to Satan and his demons. For the battle rages on, and not a physical one.

For we wrestle not against flesh and blood, but against principalities, against powers, against rulers of the darkness of this world, against spiritual wickedness in high places. Ephesians 6:12

Who are these "rulers of the darkness of this world"? Even if there was some truth to Satan's claim that the world has been given to him, what "world" are we talking about here? It's the "fallen" world that has really become his–not the earth that God created or that God intended us to inherit as His children within His kingdom. Throughout our guide, it clearly states that God is ultimately in charge. In Acts 17:29, it states that "God is the Lord of heaven and earth". Psalm 89:11 says "the heavens are yours, and the earth also is yours. The world and all its fullness–you have founded them" It is in this "fullness" of his creation that we are to find ourselves as a "new creation" (2 Corinthians 5:17) by deciding to reject Satan and that "fallen world" and embrace His kingdom.

But, can Satan have control over us? Only if we allow him to. Jesus Himself was tempted on several occasions, such as in Matthew 4, and likely he was tempted many more not recorded–since Luke 4:13 indicates that Satan departed from Jesus "for a season"–the implication being he came back to tempt Jesus in the future. The key is to resist. And, the key to resistance is our own self-control and our ability to moderate ourselves and show restraint. To give in to sin is easy because it is our natural state as a fallen being. It takes effort to resist–in fact, it takes more than that.

More Than My Earnest Effort

Romans chapter eight, my favorite chapter in our guide, told me that it would take more than my earnest effort to overcome and develop this fruit of temperance. In fact, it tells me that I am not able to do so apart from the Spirit of God. Understanding that my mind of the flesh was in opposition or "enmity" to God was difficult. Crucifying the "old man", my "body of sin", would be a formidable task.

Knowing that I came from the mind of God, that He knew me and loved me long before I was ever born, was a foundation that I could grow on. As it says in Jeremiah 1:5, "before I formed you in the womb, I knew you." There was more than simply the sexual union between a man and a women to take place for God's participation to be so strongly affirmed. God was fully involved in my life long before I entered the world. I was now determined more than ever to find out His purpose for my life.

I tested the boundaries of good and evil. Neither side seemed to cultivate in me a direction that pleased me. Discovering that we were not to eat from the tree of good and evil, therefore, allowed the light of possibilities to dance upon my spirit. We were to eat from the tree of life and I was gaining an appetite to discover what this journey was all about and exactly what would fill me up. Self-control was not on my shopping list!

Freedom

Freedom would come into my spiritual being more when the seed of temperance was cultivated into my life. Being a strong-willed individual, I would find this freedom difficult to attain. Fortunately, our guide had earned my trust as no other for the standard in which I should live. Believing was the point of entrance that my soul needed and depending on the truth as presented by love was the hope I now held onto. How could freedom bring self control? It was truly a "new" concept for me and maybe it is for you, dear reader, as well.

Nevertheless I live; yet not I, but Christ lives in me: and the life which I now live in the flesh I live by the faith of the Son of God, who loved me and gave himself for me. Galatians 2:20

My personality and my life, strangely enough, would not become a cookie-cutter, monk-like existence. This was a pleasant surprise to me while learning about life by the spirit. I had a zeal for living! I didn't develop it over the years; I'd always had it. I was pleased to find out that it was "I who lived" and that rightfully believing God who loved me *was* a preparation in me for all eternity. Loving God and committing your life to Him brings freedom, not control, which prepares your soul for all eternity.

What I've discovered is that everything God intended for me to be is what *He* was willing to develop in me. The choice was mine, but the outcome would be His. He would position me in eternity according to the faith that had developed in me in this world.

Love was teaching me that self-control would provide such freedom in me that the guide would actually position me in the Kingdom of God. I had been made for this purpose and I had the freedom to choose my way in this world or deny myself so that I could become His fulfillment of me. If you've heard anything I have written so far, you know I didn't know the way. The truth is that none of us do. As God tells Noah in Joshua 3:4, He is taking us in a way we have never been before.

The virtues that incorporate the "fruits of the spirit" are advantageous and of high caliber. They will not make us full of pride. Instead, mastering them enables us to be effective in our knowledge of Christ. God's love for His son made this available to us. Christ paid the price to reconcile my life to God according to love's guide and the decision was mine to freely choose to believe it was so.

My way had become the counterfeit of what God intended me to be. Love has gently instructed me and the Holy Spirit of God has brought life into my being far beyond my own expectations. Not only have my dreams come true, but love is preparing me for an eternity full of promises and anticipation. Who am I that God should care so about me? And what is it that love has created me to become for all eternity?

Temperance would be required to help me keep the course. Internal attacks, complacency, and heresy (to name just a few) would try to thwart my eternal soul from reaching its destination. Holding fast and rejecting all that would distort faith would require a strong dose of self-control. However, I was determined to grow up in Him–He who is more than able to do all things in me. It would be hard work. It would take obedience. Love would be the inspiration I needed.

Chapter Eleven
Meekness

If my people, which are called by my name, shall humble themselves, and pray and seek my face, and turn from their wicked ways; then will I hear from heaven, and will forgive their sin, and will heal their land. II Chronicles 7:14

Footsteps were now heard coming into the house, after the door finished creaking open. Stan was still lying on top of the bride. With his left hand, he reached up and shut off the light switch, putting them in complete darkness. The bedroom door was still locked, so whoever entered her house wouldn't have any idea she was in this predicament unless she could alert them in some way. She was frightened. He had control of her. She had no idea who had entered through her front door, and she wanted to cry out. Maybe this would be her way out of this. Or maybe he had an accomplice.

"Don't even think about making a noise," he whispered to her. "I'll kill you." Unlike before, she believed every word he said this time. The sound of the footsteps increased in volume. They were coming toward the master bedroom. Then, they heard a voice call out.

"Are you there? It's me."

She knew the voice right away–it was Lily! How did she know to show up tonight? The bride felt relief for a moment, which turned into utter dread and remorse. She did not want Lily to get involved. She would never forgive herself if her best friend got hurt. She decided to remain silent. Stan was still lying on top of her, with his head turned toward the bedroom door to hear what Lily was going to do. If they kept quiet, they both thought she would simply leave. But, she surprised them. They heard Lily touch the door handle and attempt to open it, but it was locked solid.

"I know you are both in there," Lily suddenly said, from outside the bedroom door. "If you don't come out, I'm coming in there." She turned on the light of the hallway, casting a luminous sliver from underneath the bedroom door.

There wasn't a sound. Then, Lily spoke again.

"This is your last warning," Lily announced.

There was a pause, then the bride was shocked by Stan's reaction. He got up off the bride silently and stood up to the side of the bed, facing the door. He motioned with his hand for her to stay still.

"Get out of here, Lily!" Stan yelled out.

What?! He knew her? How? Lily didn't work with them, and she had never mentioned Stan. Lily knew a lot of people, but the bride never would have guessed she had any kind of relationship with Stan. Apparently, they knew each other pretty well.

"Stan, your time is done here. Get out of this house!" Lily spoke with such authority, such power. The bride was astounded. She must have had run-ins with him before, but how could she be so confident in her words. What surprised her most was Stan's reaction and their exchange of dialogue, like this had played out before–and not in Stan's favor.

"She's...She's mine!" Stan stammered. "Why...why do you always have to interfere? I'm not giving up this time."

"Very well," said Lily. "Stand away from the door."

There was a pause.

Boom! It was a loud blast, like an explosion had gone off just outside the door. Bits of wood and metal went flying, hitting the ground in pieces. Part of the wall, bedroom door, and the doorjamb around the handle had been shattered. The door handle had been blown off. The bride jolted out of her skin. Stan stood his ground, but stared in shock at the bedroom door. From the blast, the door swung open wide. It was hard to make out Lily's image. She was standing in the entrance and, from the light in the hallway, she appeared to be a glowing, dark shadow, like a ghost in silhouette. She held something in her right hand. She flipped on the light switch. The bride couldn't believe what she saw. It was humbling, to say the least.

Lily stood in the doorway. She wore a beautiful, white, ruffled cocktail dress that went right to her knees, with a thin, red belt, red high-heeled shoes, and dangly red-earrings to match. She looked stylish and modern, but also timeless, like something from another era too. She was dressed to the nines, like she had just come from her own party. She was fully made-up, and she wore her make-up tonight like a fashion model. Her gorgeous blond hair had been done up for the evening, you could tell, but she had let it all fall out, and it was magnificent–long, shiny, and flowing. In her right hand, she held a .357 Magnum, the smoke still emanating from the barrel. She left it pointed down, but with her finger still on the trigger. She had the looks that kill, literally and figuratively.

She took three steps into the bedroom and stood at the foot of the bed. The bride was still lying on the bed, her black dress ripped from the top and still pulled up from the bottom. She stared at her in disbelief.

"Are you okay?" Lily asked her.

"I...uh...um...yes," the bride was able to mutter in response.

She turned toward Stan and spoke calmly.

"Get out of this house, Stan," Lily said. She did not raise the gun. She didn't have to.

Stan turned toward the bride. The bride did not look at him.

"I'm not done with you yet," Stan threatened.

"Get out," Lily told him again.

Without another sound but his footsteps, Stan walked past Lily and out the bedroom door. The bride watched him walk down her hallway, and turn right toward the foyer and out of sight. She heard him walk out the front door. Lily followed after him and stood at the front door, watching him go down the drive way and down the street. She closed the front door, locked the deadbolt, then turned and walked back toward the master bedroom. She placed the gun on the dresser.

The bride was sitting on the bed with her hands in her face, weeping. Lily walked over to her and knelt down in front of her.

"I love you. You are worth everything to me," said Lily, in a comforting, soothing voice.

"Lily, I'm...so...sorry."

"It's okay. Everything is alright now," she told her.

"How did you..." Lily cut her off.

"Never mind that. The important thing is that you are safe. If it's okay, I'll spend the night here with you."

The bride just nodded. Lily helped her to her feet.

"Listen..." Lily continued, looking into her eyes. "You are special to me. You always will be. I am here for you."

"Th...thank you so much. I owe you my life."

"And one day, you will know the right man for you," Lily assured her.

At that, they embraced. It felt like a mother taking care of her little daughter. When they released each other, the burden of the night hit the bride. She fell back on her bed, exhausted, with her head hitting the pillow. She closed her eyes.

Lily pulled the covers over her. In an instant, the bride was asleep. Lily sat at the edge of the bed for a minute, watching her. Then, she slowly got up and walked over to the dresser, picked up the gun, and walked out of the room, flipping the light switch as she left. In the great room, she placed the gun on an end table next to the couch, slipped out of her shoes, and laid down herself. Lily stared out of the back window at the full moon. The night sky was still full of stars.

~

Before the bride walks down the aisle to become one with her husband, many preparations have been made that will set the

The Absence of Love

stage for the rest of their lives. The analogy is much the same for the bride of Christ.

Today, as it has always been, little girls dream about their wedding day in all of its glorious detail. Many play dress-up and invariably do pretend weddings at a very young age. They can recognize the Wedding March tune by the time they are in preschool. They do tea parties and get together with other proper eligible "princesses" who know that one day their "prince" will come. The majority place great importance on the idea of finding that one true love who will share the rest of their lives with them. As that girl grows into a teenager and young adult, she begins looking at bridal magazines and websites, or watches reality TV shows based around wedding planning. She takes note of dresses, rings, and cakes that most impress her. She begins attending weddings herself, and notes what she liked and didn't like and how that wedding compared to the one she would have some day. She may even participate as a bridesmaid, getting a close taste of what the real thing may be like. She dreams over and over again about her "soul mate", the one person who would become love's ultimate definition for her. It's all part of the process, isn't it?

However, if it has nothing to do with reality, a dream can easily turn into a nightmare. I found this out the hard way. Before dreams can come true, the truth must be known. Reality, I suppose, can be many different things to different people. Here I'm not looking for a definition, but what my heart can use as a "plumb line" to hold my dreams purely in sight. When I discovered that Jesus Christ was that reality, my capacity for dreaming gained description and clarity.

More than the wedding day here, I think this chapter is about what happens before that special event and the time after. It will actually edify our daily lives if we will spend much more time clothing ourselves with love's virtues, dressing our inner being in white purity, and protecting this character with our guide's love for us. In other words, love cannot make our dreams come true if God is not in it!

Remember the overall definition that we are guided by–namely, "God is love". For a man and a woman to be in love without God in it would make Him a liar. As 1 John 5:10 says, "Anyone who believes in the Son of God has this testimony in his heart. And anyone who does not believe God has made Him out to be a liar." Marriage and a true love covenant is something that God has ordained. And through His Son, Jesus Christ, we are promised that symbolic spouse. Although the metaphor used throughout is the "Bride of Christ", even the men who are reading this book, listen up! Jesus is your primary relationship first–any earthly woman you may meet, date, fall in love with, and marry comes second to Jesus. True love, by definition, cannot exist outside of Him.

Believing takes on either this reality in our hearts or vain imaginations of our expectations of reality. I had become more familiar with the latter, but I so desired the former. Reality would have to bring my heart relationship into fellowship with our guide's definition of love. The good news is that God is more than able to do this.

Do you believe God can do anything? I think most of us do. Why then do we sometimes think that God cannot be in fellowship with us, that He is simply some distant Being who put the world into motion, but then wants nothing more to do with us. This is what the Deists think, and many self-professed "believers" are of that persuasion without realizing that's what it's called. Many today would agree that, though they say there is a God, that He doesn't intervene in the affairs of human beings and simply watches from afar–or worse, doesn't watch or doesn't care at all. And, those same people would say that it's pointless to pray because, although He may hear us, we are, after all, lowly humans who can't possibly have personal communication with such an intelligent Being. They believe that God cannot or will not speak to us, and has no influence over us or the world He created. Does that sound like love to you?

Apart from God We Can Do Nothing

I've had to do a bit more preparation to address "meekness"

the next "fruit of the spirit", in this chapter. Meekness is also translated as gentleness. Humility (the condition of being humble) and submission (the state of being submissive or compliant) are also synonyms of meekness.

The selection of II Chronicles 7:14 at the beginning of this chapter emphasizes the relevance of humility:

If my people, which are called by my name, shall humble themselves, and pray and seek my face, and turn from their wicked ways; then will I hear from heaven, and will forgive their sin, and will heal their land.

There is so much meat in this scripture. The essence of these words addresses our heart. In this verse, God is speaking to His chosen people, Israel. In the verse that precedes it, God addresses King Solomon, in rule at that time, about some of the things that could happen to Israel if they continue in their rebellion, such as to "shut up heaven so that there will be no rain" or "to command the locusts to devour the land". These potential "curses" are followed up by the actions that need to be taken (the "ifs") to receive the glorious blessings promised to them (the "thens")–such as the "healing of their land".

However, it can be argued that the promises made to Israel here can be applied to Christians today. Are you a child of God (one of "His people")? Have you humbled yourself before Him? Do you pray? Do you "seek His face"? What does that mean anyway? When we have a personal relationship with someone, we want to speak with them "face to face", as Moses did. We want to be in their presence, and be able to see them physically. The countenance on one's face expresses that person's true feelings and true desires. As a metaphor in our guide, seeking His face means to want what He wants, to value what He values, to seek His heart, not your own (or not just what God can do for us), and ultimately to look to put your time and effort in the things that God cares about (such as developing the "fruits" we have been discussing), not the things that this fallen world values. Did you turn from your "wicked ways"? We can turn from sin, but that doesn't mean we won't keep committing it and require forgiveness time and time again.

These are all things that we are commanded to do in various scriptures in the New Testament as well. And, although we are not under the same specific threats and curses that befell Israel at that time, we are told that Jesus is "the way, the truth, and the life"–without Him, "no one" can get to His father in heaven. The promises of "forgiveness of sins" and "healing" are ultimately fulfilled in the "land" of the heavenly realm when we accept Jesus.

But, what does it really mean to be "humble"?

Humility

My research has uncovered that, in the pre-Christian era, humility was something absolutely not wanted. The definition of humility apart from God reads like this: affliction, oppression, put down, a bestowing of labor upon, poor, and depressed. Even today, an acceptable synonym of being humble is being "submissive", which itself has its own identity problems as a positive quality. It's when "submission' turns into abuse that it becomes a detriment. Considering they rhyme, many people hear "meek" as "weak". The negative connotations around the idea of humility persist today. No wonder many of us aren't keen about being humble. The antonyms of humility, such as assertiveness, pretentiousness, and being proud or egotistical, are qualities more apt to be sought by many of today's generation who are not "seeking His face."

When one's heart is in right order and God comes on the scene, everything changes. If meekness is the result of abuse or oppression, that isn't love. And again, love does not operate properly apart from God. When we turn from our "wicked ways" and towards God in humility, we are acknowledging that an all-powerful, all-knowing, all-loving personal Being is worthy of all the reverence, admiration, respect, and worship that we can offer Him. That is what humility is. And, it is taking place where love can make a way that we have never been before–in our hearts! In Proverbs 11:2, it says that "when pride comes then comes disgrace.

But with humility comes wisdom". Be humble and be wise, says our guide!

Is God Humble?

We know our guide asks us humans to be humble, but, as we are to seek His face and be more like Him, then we can ask: how is God humble? It seems a strange description to place on an omniscient, omnipotent God. However, when we understand the definition of humility as "gentleness", it begins to make sense. God's gentle spirit manifests itself in His mercy and unending ability to offer grace, forgiveness, and clemency to us, his beloved.

God chose to regard and associate with the poor and the lowly (Psalm 138:6), rather than the high and the mighty of humanity. In Psalm 113:5-6, it says that God "humbles himself to behold the things in heaven and on earth." Also, since God is love, and love is neither proud nor selfish–two opposites of humility–then it follows that God is humble indeed.

God's example of humility is also shown in many of the prominent leaders throughout our guide, such as Abraham, Isaac, Moses, and Gideon. However, the prime example of humility is found in none other than Jesus Christ Himself.

Jesus emptied himself, taking the form of a servant, being born in the likeness of men. And being found in human form he humbled himself and became obedient unto death, even death on the cross. Philippians 2:6-8

Throughout his ministry, Jesus exalted the poor and lowly, the oppressed and the burdened. He told the multitudes in his famous sermon on the mount that the "meek" were "blessed" and that they would "inherit the earth". In Matthew 11:29, Jesus describes Himself when he says "I am meek (gentle) and humble of heart." Finally, in His suffering and death, Jesus was the picture of humility. He offered himself up, without pride, without arrogance, without ego, as a willing sacrifice and the ultimate example of what it means to be humble. He was always seeking the presence and the will of His eternal Father in heaven–seeking His face and "only doing what the Father does" (John 5:19).

As stated before, meekness is also a characteristic of wisdom. And God is of course the ultimate in wisdom "that comes from heaven". He is omniscient, knowing all. James says it this way, comparing that wisdom to meekness:

But the wisdom that comes from heaven is first of all pure; then peace-loving, considerate, meek, full of mercy and good fruit, impartial and sincere. James 3:17

This verse offers additional descriptions of the qualities of God: pure, peaceful, considerate, merciful. Again, being meek is wrapped up in that description, all which is equated with being wise. It'll result in "good fruit", again tying into our growth and development as Christians.

Commitment to Meekness

Meekness is much more than gentleness of manner. It is a grace that requires each of us to totally submit ourselves to the way of love and realize apart from it we can do nothing. Meekness gives us an opportunity through love to preserve our spirit while we continue preparing for the wedding feast. As it says in Zephaniah 2:3, we are commanded to "seek righteousness" at the same time we are to "seek meekness". The two are equal goals to strive for. In Zephaniah, it's offered as a warning to avoid "the Lord's anger." That's probably something we should pay attention to!

Our commitment to meekness pre-supposes that God will protect, care for, and preserve our hearts for all eternity. It is more than I have ever given meekness credit for in life. Father, forgive me! Let me turn from my way and yield willingly to You. In my heart, I know I am totally dependent upon love. Love never fails!

Chapter Twelve
Kindness

But when the kindness and love of God our Savior appeared, he saved us, not because of righteous things we have done, but because of his mercy. Titus 3:4

The main ceremony room had filled up, and there was quite a buzz going on, with people awaiting the music to start and the bride to walk the aisle. The bride herself had been whisked away mentally by the memory of that night when Lily had to come to her rescue. Despite the tough, direct manner in which she disposed of Stan that night, she remained the peaceful, gentle, kind friend that she had always known her to be. And, she didn't judge her–she simply forgave her. Oh, she also had some stern words for her the next day, but it was because she cared about the bride so much and wanted the best for her. Her compassion, mercy, and love for her knew no bounds.

The same could be said for the groom. However, there was a big difference. Though Lily was her best friend, her guide, and her confidante, nothing could replace the man she was about to marry. There were many before him who tried to woo her, even took advantage of her and manipulated her affections, and others that she even pursued herself, but she realized she was wrong about what she was looking for. She didn't realize what made her life complete until she met him. He had many admirers even before she knew him, but also many who did not like him–even despised him. And, when she met him at that party, she didn't know that, in a few short months, he was about to go through something so horrible–it was gut-wrenching for her to watch it happen, and she didn't suffer the physical pain he did. She could not imagine what it was for him.

It all started when she decided to "date" him. Date really isn't the right word, but that's the word we have in contemporary society to describe their early relationship. It was more like she became his "follower", but not in any subservient way. He admired, respected, and, especially, loved her more than she could ever love him. She went along with him to various mission trips that he led. She became his "right hand" person so to speak–his hands and feet to spread his message of compassion and love and to assist in the medical, food, and shelter communities he was building for those who had no hope before they knew him. It was amazing what he was able to accomplish with so little tangible supplies and finances. It seemed the resources and the money multiplied on their own–whenever they needed something, it was there, and always just the right amount.

He had a small group of people that were part of his team at that time. He went to many places in the world that had been rejected or considered too difficult to deal with by others who were doing similar work as him–places that had the poorest of the poor living out in the street, countries and cities ruled by a corrupt government, even small towns and communities where violence and murder were a way of life. No place was off-limits for him–the deepest parts of Africa; the most remote and neglected areas of North and South America, Europe, and Asia; even the most dangerous terrorist areas of the Middle East.

But, it was a particular missionary trip one spring that the bride, Lily, and several of his team accompanied the groom on that would be like no other trip he had gone on before–or ever would again.

~

Most of us have met what we would term "kind" individuals, haven't we? They are generally appreciated in special moments of our lives. Kindness is traced by definition, however, to the motivation of one's heart. What is behind the kind act or the kind word that someone gives another?

Everyone is familiar with the saying, "I'll scratch your back if you'll scratch mine." Has anyone ever done an act of kindness for you only to have you think: "I wonder what they will want in return?" This is the motivation side of kindness that is rarely dealt with.

Experience will teach anyone looking for love that the kindness one may have demonstrated the night before is not necessarily the kind motivation the heart illustrates the next morning! Get the picture? I paid a very high price to learn about counterfeit kindness, so it is with some degree of my own errant way that this life lesson is discussed.

Kindness from someone's actions or words can start genuinely enough, or feel genuine, when it is something that you want or get satisfaction from initially. However, as time goes on, when a relationship becomes one-sided or you get behind the true motivation of those "kind" deeds, it can deteriorate into abuse or "feeling used." Condemnation, guilt, and bitterness can begin to set in, both in yourself and toward the person who was the object or origin of the initial kindness. Most can relate to these feelings, especially guilt, which is a tactic of the devil, the enemy of love.

What's in a Word?

It's interesting to note that the origins of the word "kindness" are uniquely connected to the word "use" or "usefulness." When Paul provides those "fruits of the spirit" in Galatians 5:22, the Greek word for kindness (*chrestotes*) in that list means "useful" or "fit for use." In Paul's letter, it refers to a gift from God that is useful for ourselves and others. It is like a "tool" that, when used correctly, can build up our relationships and nurture them. But, like any tool, when used incorrectly, it can destroy and undermine the integrity of those same relationships.

Apart from God, "kindness" is a tool in the enemy's hand. It is my ardent hope that, for those who have entered into this covenant of love, that they will be able to see the motivation of "kindness", in themselves and others, and be able to detect it as either a tool used in opposition to our Lord or as the "fruit of the spirit" that Paul talks about in Galatians.

The Hebrew definition of kindness is even more enlightening. Many references in the Old Testament of our guide refer to "kindness" in several aspects. The primary Hebrew word for "kindness" is *chesed*, but it meant more than simply what being "kind" means in English today. To show "chesed" was central to Jewish ethics and Jewish theology.

For example, in Proverbs 31:26, wisdom and kindness are related in the description of what a good woman is: "She opens her mouth with wisdom, and on her tongue is the law of kindness". Kindness is the "law" or what should "rule" in how we speak to each other. One who speaks with kindness is a "wise" speaker.

In several scriptures in Genesis and throughout the Old Testament, it is God's kindness or the kindness of others that is either shown or sought in the yearnings of Abraham, Abimelech, Joseph, Joshua, Ruth, Samuel, and many others. In almost every instance, it is not just about words, but about putting kindness into action. It's easy to throw a kind word someone's way, which is important, but can we turn it into a kind deed? Many times, this effort takes sacrifice and gets at the heart of loving someone–because we want to show them. It's kindness that God "shows" His people time and time again in our guide.

In the New Testament, the scripture from our guide that starts this chapter sheds additional light on the concept of kindness:

But when the kindness and love of God our Savior appeared, he saved us, not because of righteous things we had done, but because of his mercy. Titus 3:4

Here, God has saved us not because of our works, but because He is a merciful God. As it says in Romans 2:4, , it's "His kindness that leads to repentance." We are forgiven, and we are repentant of our wrongdoings, because of God's kindness and His mercy. In turn, when His kindness blossoms in us, we can be forgiving to others who wrong us in some way.

Application is the "how" in motivation. God's motivation for His people is out of kindness and love–pure and simple. In fact, the word "kindness" became intertwined with the concept of love like no other fruit of the spirit. In English, the compound word "lovingkindness" or simply "love" became a translation of the Hebrew word "chesed". Kindness and love come to mean the same thing in many iterations of the word. Of all the fruits, kindness seems to be the best example of what love means, or how it is expressed or displayed.

Though most of us know what it means, it is what we don't know about kindness that has allowed the fiery arrows of the enemy of love to not only aim at our hearts (the application of kindness), but to hit the target. This enemy is motivated to allow kindness to be misused or even to turn into abuse, resulting in the separation of us from the lover of our soul, Jesus Christ. My incentive is to bring the inspiration necessary to disarm this enemy. By bringing this into the light, we will not so easily underestimate our adversary. Of course, the adversary we speak of here, the enemy of our guide, is Satan himself. In a battle of wits, the devil can do damage if we are not always on the watch.

I have forgiven in the sight of Christ for your sake, in order that Satan might not outwit us. For we are not unaware of his schemes. II Corinthians 2:10b-11

Like Kind(ness) from the Potter

Incorporating "unearthed" information about kindness can and will protect love. In both Isaiah 64 and Jeremiah 18 in our guide, the image of the potter is used to describe how God forms and shapes man. God formed man out of the dust of the earth and then continues to transform him through His spirit, like a potter forming his pottery out of clay. When we are in the hands of the potter, we can be shaped, formed, and even used by His gracious and compassionate spirit. This will produce the fruit of kindness in us. When this fruit matures, it will produce the seed of kindness that when planted in others will begin to produce "according to its kind" (Genesis 1:12). Remember! This is only possible because our guide describes God as slow to anger and abounding in love and great kindness, which I admit has been contrary to my own existence.

There have been times, however, when my life has produced random acts of kindness that surprised me. One instance was when my youngest son, Christopher, was too young to have developed a reasoning mind. I believe he was about two years old. The family was sitting around the kitchen table with Granny. Little innocent (or not so innocent) Christopher was sitting in my lap. Without any warning, he lifted his hand and slapped me across the face. I don't remember why, or even if there was a problem. When you experience something like this, especially from a little child, for many people, it is spontaneous and natural to respond in like manner. A slap back is how many parents would punish a hurtful action such as this, even from a non-reasoning two-year-old. If time can stand still, it did on that day. Everything traveled in slow motion and all eyes were upon me, shocked as I was with this inappropriate action from my son.

I am reminded of Jesus's own admonishment of the "eye for an eye, tooth for a tooth" mentality when he said in Matthew 5:39 to "turn the other cheek" when you are smitten on one cheek. Revenge seems still to be today's prevalent and "fair" way to deal with people who wrong you, but how much further would we get to show kindness and mercy instead?

It turns out that hurting my son's flesh as he had mine didn't even occur to me. There are verses in our guide that endorse discipline of children when it is warranted and effective, such as Proverbs 13:24 ("the one who loves their children is careful to discipline them"). However, "discipline" has many forms. In the case of my son's slapping me, I think simple instruction was the best bet. So, teaching him with love is what I did.

Preparation Work

Honestly, God's mercy towards us does the same thing because of His great kindness. Why I don't respond regularly with this kindness is regrettable, but alludes to my sinful nature. Developing awareness to live differently is the seed of kindness that was planted in me when I chose to abide in Him. He continues to court me through His grace, favor, and mercy, assuring me that with Him all things are possible, including His kindness in me.

You see, this is the preparation work I've written of throughout this text, the lead I asked to take of you in the introduction–the truths God purposed in life for His eternal Bride. Please understand that it is His zeal and good sense in love that will accomplish this in you and me. He is preparing us for the wedding feast. He is the lover of our soul.

Listen! My lover! Look! Here he comes. Song of Songs 2:8

Chapter Thirteen
Goodness

Let them give thanks to the Lord for his unfailing love and his wonderful deeds for men. For he satisfies the thirsty soul, and fills the hungry soul with goodness. Psalm 107:8-9

The groom went with his team, including Lily, the bride, and about 50 others, to a part of the Middle East not known to many outside of this area. It was a small village with hundreds of people. These were the poorest of the poor.

For those families who had jobs or a way of supporting themselves, they were able to just get by, having barely enough money for food, a few rags for clothes, and makeshift shacks that simply provided some relief from the blazing sun or the torrential rain storms. If high winds hit this area, many were left homeless and would have to rebuild from scratch.

For other families, the government provided essentials through air drops or distribution to a central post office miles away for those who could make it there, deal with the corruption, and fight for a few items for their family. Because of its remote location, delivery of anything by foot or vehicle was difficult. It was mountainous, and the roads were primitive at best–at worst, there were no roads and you had to make sure you had a good map, if you could get one.

When the groom and his team arrived, most did not know what to expect. They were taken aback by the wretched conditions

The Absence of Love

of the people and how they were living. Many were starving to death. If they weren't starving, they had communicable diseases that spread amongst the village quickly unless the afflicted were isolated from the others. Food was scarce and medicine was scarcer. Some were getting by with a couple meals a week, which mainly consisted of bread and rice, sometimes supplemented with fava beans, green vegetables like cabbage or spinach, and, for the more fortunate ones, lamb, chicken, and eggs. Some had their own simple gardens to grow food themselves, but were mainly dependent on the rain or pulled water from a nearby tributary of the Tigris River. There was a large city several miles away at which many worked or sold their wares, if they were healthy enough to get there. A few had animal-drawn carts or bicycles, but most travelled on foot.

The majority of the villagers welcomed the groom and his team with open arms. Some were skeptical and, for those who had a working relationship with the government, even resentful. But, once the groom was able to set up shop and begin speaking to them and dealing with their needs, many were won over. The groom had always said that, to teach someone to be compassionate, you have to show compassion to them first, regardless of how you are treated. He always said he learned that from his father, and that he wanted to do what his father would have him to do. He also always treated their physical conditions first, before moving on to teach them about love, compassion, patience, kindness, and all the attributes that he believed anyone needed to live a fulfilling life.

It was a novel concept to many, particularly those in this village who were used to having to fend for themselves. The mortality rate was very high in this area–the life expectancy was not much past 50, and it wasn't unheard of for many children from the same family to have died before they reached the age of 13. Selfishness was a way of life for people in this region.

The villagers were amazed at how this group operated and how the groom treated them–mainly, with respect and dignity. They had never seen that from outsiders, including the government officials who would occasionally visit. They were used to being looked at with scorn and contempt, as if they weren't good enough to be kept alive.

The groom's team gave the village basic food and medicine, simple items that people in wealthier countries took for granted. During the first week, many were brought back to health and given hope and a reason to live. The team soon ran out of the food and medicine they had brought, but still the people kept coming, wanting to be healed and fed. Then, the inexplicable began happening.

The villagers began listening to what the groom had to say–his words of encouragement, of peace, of kindness, of love. He spoke in metaphor all the time, explaining his concepts in simple stories filled with symbolism. In some cases, people could understand easily. In other cases, they asked questions and really had to think about what he was saying to get to the deeper meaning. For those who believed and trusted in what the groom told them, they did not even need the medicine that was being distributed. All who had diseases or afflictions in some form were cured or healed, without any explanation. Blind people were suddenly able to see again. The deaf and mute could hear and speak again. People with psychosis became sane. People with seemingly incurable skin conditions and other diseases completely lost their symptoms. The crippled who were brought to the groom on stretchers were able to walk again. Others from surrounding villages and from miles around got word of the groom and began coming. It was an incredible chain of events over those next several weeks.

The bride was astounded. Although she had heard of similar things occurring on the groom's previous trips, she had not experienced it herself firsthand before. Her trust in him grew to a much deeper level, and her love for him and faithfulness to him knew no bounds.

However, she became concerned about the reaction of a certain group of local people to the events occurring. Apparently, word had spread to the local government, and even to wider branches, that the groom was causing the people to rely on him for their basic needs rather than the government or those in charge in the city. They were threatened by this mysterious man who seemed to have great power and influence. The government was losing control over its people. The officials in charge needed to put an end to it.

Unbeknownst to the bride (but known by the groom and Lily, she would later learn), the government dispatched military personnel to the village to stop the groom and his rebellious actions. The bride also didn't know that there was a traitor on the groom's team. The government had contracted with this person to report what the groom was doing. This traitor would be the government's star witness to bring him down.

The bride never would have guessed what was going to occur over the course of the next twenty-four hours.

~

In today's society, most do not prefer a world that is simply "black and white". The proverbial "gray" seems to be the preference of the majority. I agree with "gray" as an alternative to aligning ourselves with certain extremes, or when discussing our opinions or strategies for sociology, business, psychology, art and literature, and many other subjects. But the alarming trend over the past few decades is that many people take the concept of "gray" itself to an extreme. I think today's society views concepts like "good" and "bad", "right" and "wrong", and even "truth" and "lie" as simply that–concepts that are up for debate. What is good or goodness? What is evil? A long time ago, when people lived by certain established standards, these ideas were clearer to the average person. Today, the meanings are blurred.

Of course, the guide I have been discussing, the Bible, is what I believe will always be our standard to live by that defines these "concepts" well. And, if we have a relationship with Jesus Christ and are guided by the Holy Spirit, we can discern what God's will and purpose are in many situations in our life without having to constantly question whether we are doing the "right" thing, simply because the rest of society says there is no one way to approach an answer to the questions that trouble us. So, let's take a look at this way of thinking that takes gray to the extreme, called "postmodernism".

Gray to the Extreme

Postmodernism is a concept used by sociologists, philosophers, and others to describe a way of thinking that has become very popular in the world (particularly in the United States) over the last generation. It is an approach to reality and defining ethics and morality that has had a significant effect on art and literature, education, psychology, law, science, the study of history, and people's view of religion. It's impossible to pigeonhole it, really, into one single "belief" as one of its tenets is that there is no absolute "truth" or belief system any longer. It's not a "worldview" – it's a "personview" – what each individual person believes or thinks is what goes. There is no standard any longer. Quite scary, really!

Many writers in the 20th century have promoted this concept and continue to today. It is pervasive on most television shows, Hollywood movies, and stories of fiction. Its origins are found in the philosophies of Frederick Nietzsche, Martin Heidegger, Karl Marx, and Sigmund Freud. In its attitudes toward truth and good/evil, it shares the thinking of the New Age movement, with proponents like Shirley MacClaine, who has said "I think of life itself now as a wonderful play that I've written for myself, and so my purpose is to have the utmost fun playing my part." This is typical of a worldview in which what you define for yourself is all that matters. God has no part in this "play".

What is "Modernism"?

But, if it's "post" (meaning "to come after"), what is modernism? It's one of the three "epochs" of philosophical worldviews that contemporary philosophers have grouped human history: premodernism, modernism, and postmodernism. This grouping has been established in the latter half of the 20th century, and it's important to understand to see where many would define what "goodness" is and from where it derives.

The premodern period, dated from the beginning of time to about 1650, was based upon revealed knowledge from authoritative sources. In premodern times, it was believed that ultimate "truth" could be known and the way to this knowledge was through direct revelation. This direct revelation was generally assumed to come from God. In many ways, we need to get back to this way of thinking!

Modernism, dated from 1650 to about 1950, defined two new ways of "knowing" something: one was knowing through the senses (sometimes called "empiricism") which gradually became our way of study through the scientific method, using observation and experimentation. The second way of "knowing" was through reason or logic using the human mind and intelligent thought. Frequently, science and reason worked in conjunction with one another. As a result, the shift of power for authority moved away from the church (which wasn't a bad thing in many cases when those in power were corrupt). Political figures (such as kings) and learned men (such as university scholars) took over as the primary sources of authority. Often, God or some kind of religious perspective was integrated into these modern authority sources, but the church no longer enjoyed the privileged power position it once held.

What is "Postmodernism"?

Postmodernism, then, is a recent reaction to modernism which many people today, although they may not even know it, now subscribe to. It states that we all create our own reality. God tends to be out of the picture. Should God exist, he certainly has nothing to say about what we should believe or how we should behave. Many postmodernists distrust the ability for modern technology to give us the answers we seek, and, in a sense, I believe they are correct. The modernist way will never prove or demonstrate who God really is, how our mind truly works, what makes something "right" or "wrong", what happens after we die, or many other of life's mysteries.

Postmodernists believe that it is not truth that matters, but simply our choices, our preferences, and our feelings. Emotions, feelings, intuition, and reflection are now the most important factors. It's not about what "I know"; it's about what "I feel". In fact, one person's choice or preference is no better than another's.

Postmodernism does not trust any authority, dogma, or standard – and our guide would definitely fall into that category for the postmodernist. All moral values are relative. Each person or culture develops their own moral values. The important question is not "Is it right?" but "What will it do for me?" It teaches that we are shaped by our culture, and therefore taking personal responsibility is not as important anymore.

Many people have moved on in their personal worldview to either "modernism" or "postmodernism" (or a combination of the two), but the foundations of the "premodern" era, where answers to the bigger spiritual questions can be found by revelation and God's word, are still true today. However, the empirical way of knowing through our "senses" does play a part in the spiritual definition of "goodness", as we shall see.

Good to the Senses

Love's goodness seems to require, in fact has built in, a sensory system clearly demonstrating good to our brain that is not to be ignored. The following scripture seems to be a warning to the postmodernist way of thinking:

Woe to those who call evil good and good evil. Isaiah 5:20a

Our guide indicates that there are clear definitions of "good" and "evil", and we are being told not to confuse the two, or "woe" (distress, calamity, misery, misfortune) will come upon us. The plumb line positioned in me finds some comfort in realizing that the senses God has created in me contain this divine perceptibility.

Using the scripture that opens this chapter as an example, goodness has specific definitions aligned with the senses. The Hebrew word for goodness is *tovati*. The root is *tovah* (or shortened even to *tov*), meaning good, well-pleasing, proper, prosperous, convenient, and morally correct. On one hand, it refers to what is good, pleasant, and agreeable to the senses. What our eyes, ears, taste, and touch senses as pleasing or "good" is good. With our human senses, we can experience "goodness". This "goodness" can also be explained as agreeable and pleasant to man's higher, sensuous, or intellectual nature, and to ethics. Psalms says it this way:

You are my Lord. I have no good apart from You. Psalm 16:2

There's no guess work here. The psalmist David is saying that "no good" exists apart from God. He is the author of good, and has given it to us. As God has created man in His image (before the fall of man happened with sin), goodness is all from a good, moral, benevolent point of view. His!

For example, murder requires a moral judgment in us that designates what the majority believes as bad. I selected this notorious crime believing that, regardless of our differences and cultures, that most (even the postmodernists) still believe cold blooded, premeditated murder is wrong. I was looking for the agreement of the masses, which seems so difficult in today's world to come by. I did this because I want to create the same kind of unity regarding goodness. This word has become so grayed that I think it necessary to do so and our guide verifies this belief. It is helpful to look at all of Isaiah 5:20 now.

Woe to those who call evil good and good evil, who put darkness for light and light for darkness, who put bitter for sweet and sweet for bitter. Isaiah 5:20

Using the perspective that there is no gray when it comes to "good" and "evil" becomes clearer now with the comparison of those opposites to light with dark and bitter with sweet. Everyone would agree that light and dark are opposites, since, using our eyes, we can see that difference clearly. Additionally, using our universal taste buds, everyone can taste the difference between sweet and bitter. Those opposites should never be confused. The "sensing" of good and evil should be just as clear to us, and we better know the difference and not call them their opposites or the results will be disastrous in a spiritual sense.

Empathy as Goodness

Goodness needs to be clearly understood. What it is beyond the belief system you and I have formed personally is compulsory. Before doing this, however, I felt led to ask some people close to my realm of influence this question: "What does good mean to you"? My daughter Christy had a very interesting response.

After a time of reflection, Christy said, simply, "empathy". Goodness meant "empathy" to her – to think outside of ourselves upon someone less fortunate and identify with that person's feelings. She proceeded to tell a story about an elderly woman she would see in the streets of Dartford, England when Christy was shopping and running her errands. The elderly woman was bent over with ankles twice the normal size. Christy wondered what her life was like and, with tears in her eyes heard only by me over the phone, she had questioned silently that day in Dartford and again now with me: why was there no one to help her? How had this women's life come to this? How come she didn't have anyone to help her? Empathy!

Finally, all of you be of one mind, having compassion for one another; love as brothers, be tenderhearted, be courteous. 1 Peter 3:8

Empathy is about compassion and love. And it's the Lord's goodness that he wants to pass on to us, expecting us to be empathetic to our fellow man because of it. The next verse shows that my daughter was on to something there with her comparison of goodness and empathy, particularly to the poor and lowly.

You, O God, provided from Your goodness for the poor. Psalm 68:10

After speaking on the phone for quite a long time, I asked Christy: "Do you have anything else you would like to tell me about what goodness means to you?" She said: "I'm making egg salad and that's real good!" That speaks more to the sense of taste, I suppose, but also to the sense of smell of good food.

They ate to the full and were well-nourished; they reveled in your great goodness. Nehemiah 9:25

Can You Smell It?

Strangely enough, the sense of smell is also required to know what "good" is. Through my research, I had discovered this pleasant, agreeable scripture from our guide. The reference to smells is found in several places, the first one here in Genesis:

And the Lord smelled a soothing aroma. Then the Lord said in His heart, "I will never again curse the ground for man's sake...nor will I again destroy every living thing as I have done. Genesis 8:21

Similar to the love covenant we have been describing throughout this book, the Lord made a new covenant with mankind here, and specifically to Noah, to never again destroy the entire world as He did in the flood. The "soothing aroma" He smelled came from the clean animals and birds that Noah burned as a burnt offering for the Lord. This sense of the burnt offering being a pleasant aroma is paralleled in the New Testament in a couple places. One is in Ephesians.

And walk in love, as Christ also has loved us and given Himself for us, an offering and a sacrifice to God for a sweet-smelling aroma. Ephesians 5:2

Most of us have a special perfume that we like the fragrance of. That's good, isn't it? There are of course many opinions about the different brands available and how our sense of smell captures the aroma. There is perhaps no battle here, just personal preference, but let us define even further the sense of smell referenced to "good".

How good and pleasant it is when brothers live together in unity! It is like precious oil poured on the head, running down on the beard, running down on Aaron's beard, down upon the collar of his robes. Psalm 133:2

Can you smell it? And listen further as it is described in the following verse of this Psalm what this scent is to denote to the plumb line in us of goodness.

It is as if the dew of Hermon were falling on Mount Zion. For there the Lord bestows his blessing, even life forevermore. Psalm 133:3

Blessings are generally met with the approval of all humanity when it occurs in their lives. When the Lord bestows His good blessing in our lives, there is nothing temporary about it. It is the kind of good I seek because all that dazzles, or appears to be "good", may indeed be false and does not satisfy in the same way. This blessing comes with the fragrance that brings "life forevermore". It is eternal!

So empathy, smell, and taste are what "goodness" expressed to our only daughter. Honestly, I don't think empathy was even on my radar screen as a definition of "good".

Can You See It?

The attachment of "goodness" to the eyes is both a blessing and a curse in our guide. It shows precisely why it is important to route out counterfeit goodness.

When the woman saw that the fruit of the tree was good for food and pleasing to the eye, and also desirable for gaining wisdom, she took some and ate it. She also gave some to her husband, who was with her, and he ate it. Genesis 3:6

What happened to the senses in that moment that began a deception that often perverts goodness? Eve saw the apple as "good for food", yet the act of eating it became the supreme act of disobedience that was the opposite of "goodness". It launched evil into the world. What about other things that are pleasing to the eye, such as the nude form of a handsome man or a beautiful woman? Adam and Eve had no need for clothes when they were in the garden of Eden. But, as soon as they sinned, they felt aware and ashamed of their nakedness. They felt compelled to cover themselves up and hide, as physical response against their spiritual wrongdoing. However, when that nude form is not the spouse of a married person and it is placed before their eyes, temptation results. When used the way God has intended them, nudity and sexual intercourse are good. But, when they become temptation to sin, they are a perversion of "goodness". Can you feel the battle? Can you see it?

Pride and Prejudice

The next story from our guide, from the prophet Isaiah, addresses these questions with a result that still has my mind in a bit of a quandary.

At the time Merodach-Baladan son of Babylon sent Hezekiah letters and a gift, because he had heard of his illness and recovery.

*Hezekiah received the envoys gladly and showed them what was in his storehouses—the silver, the gold, the spices, the fine oil, his entire armory and everything round among his treasures. There was nothing in his palace or in all his kingdom that Hezekiah did not show them. Then Isaiah the prophet went to King Hezekiah and asked, "What did those men say, and where did they come from?" "From a distant land, "Hezekiah replied. "They came to me from Babylon." The prophet asked, "What did they see in your palace?" They saw everything in my palace, "Hezekiah said. "There is nothing among my treasures that I did not show them." Then Isaiah said to Hezekiah, "Hear the word of the Lord Almighty: The time will surely come when everything in your palace, and all that your fathers have stored up until this day, will be carried off to Babylon. Nothing will be left, says the Lord. And some of your descendants, your own flesh and blood who will be born to you, will be taken away, and they will become eunuchs in the palace of the King of Babylon. "The word of the Lord you have spoken is **good**." Hezekiah replied. For he thought, "There will be peace and security in my lifetime."*

What? To anyone reading this scripture, from Isaiah 39, who heard this as Hezekiah did, please explain! How can it be "good" to have everything you own and "your own flesh and blood" be "taken away from you" and serve in the "palace of the King of Babylon", notorious idol worshippers. And, to top it off, apparently to have their sexual organs removed to be turned into "eunuchs"? Huh? How is that "good"? That puts quite a spin on the definition of that word, doesn't it?

Hezekiah was one of Judah's most faithful kings. He worked hard throughout his reign to stamp out idol worship and to purify the worship of the true God at Jerusalem's Temple. Merodach-Baladan was a Babylonian prince who was planning a revolt against Assyria and was trying to form an alliance with the King of Judah, Hezekiah. Why would the Lord do this to Hezekiah? And stranger still, why would the king call this "good"?

Why King Hezekiah decided to show this Babylonian Prince "everything" in the first place leaves me looking like a deer

The Absence of Love

caught in head lights. My soul screams out, "What"? I believe it has something to do with the king being prideful, as in "pride cometh before a fall". This is actually an abbreviated version of Proverbs 16:18, which in full says "Pride cometh before destruction, and a haughty spirit before the fall." and it did. The Babylonians became Judah's next threat, and they, not the Assyrians, would conquer the king's city.

My comprehension difficulty comes when the king's response to Isaiah's strong word of impending trouble is read through his senses as "good". Listen, my brothers and sisters who have travelled this journey with me–we can neither call nor express "good" for what is "bad". Isaiah had already warned the king not to trust Babylon. That in itself should have communicated a strong warning to Hezekiah when Babylon showed up. It didn't! The King showed him "everything" in the palace, giving the prince motivation beyond alliance.

Remember the concept of "motivation" in our study on kindness in the previous chapter? It delineated the difference between what edified self from a response that was generated out of divine influence.

You may be familiar with the old joke about the flood waters rising at a man's house, so he goes to his rooftop for safety. As the waters continue to rise, he prays to God, pleading with Him to save the man from being drowned. Someone in a row boat comes his way, but the man fails to get in it. "The Lord will protect me" he says, and refuses to get in the boat. A little later, a larger motor boat with several people on board comes by. "Get in our boat", they say to the man. Again, the man refuses. "No. The Lord will save me." Time passes, and the water is almost to the top of his roof. A helicopter comes by and the people inside throw down a ladder to the man, pleading with him to climb the ladder to get in the helicopter. Still, the man refuses the help. "I have prayed to the Lord. He will save me." Eventually, the man is overcome with water and he drowns. He meets the Lord in heaven and the man says: "Lord, I was faithful to you and prayed to you for help. Why didn't you save me?" And God responded: "Well, I tried. I sent you a row boat, a motor boat, and a helicopter. What did you expect?"

God's messenger Isaiah was a prophet. Without going into detail about what all that means, understand that God is more than able to convey to each of us what it takes to watch over us, care for us, and, most of all, love us. What do we expect?

Isaiah warned the king, and in great detail shared with him, but as though the prince was a dear loved one of the king, instead of the "enemy." Hezekiah showed him all the nation's blessings that he had attained, no doubt from love. In turn, he didn't realize he was also showing his enemy all that he would give to him.

But the question still remains: how is the prophecy given to Hezekiah considered "good" in the king's assessment? In this case, it seems the concept of "good" here is that Hezekiah "sees" or understands that the Lord is being right and just in punishing him. "Good" represents the king's agreement with God's decision to punish him. Hezekiah believed he had sinned, that he bragged about his treasures, and deserved to be punished. It is clear that the punishment would be generations later, not immediate, which was a relief to Hezekiah. The king thought the punishment could have been much worse, and that God was showing His mercy and loving kindness in this case. God was granting him peace and prosperity ("security") during his reign, as the prophecy would not come true until years later. Even in calamity and suffering, we can still find evidence of God's goodness.

The Enemy

It's in this place that I want to add to our foundation of good the importance of knowing our enemy once again. Satan is still alive and well in this world. In 1 John 4:3, he is mentioned as "the Antichrist, which you have heard was coming, and is now already in the world." He shows up in many different forms. He is the "king of the bottomless pit" (Revelation 9:11) who "transforms himself into an angel of light" (2 Corinthians 11:14). He is also the "father of lies" (John 8:44) who "deceives the whole world" (Revelation 12:9).

Good presents itself as an imposter and we can use the good senses love assembled in each of us just as was done in Adam and Eve. But still, they missed it! Let's not follow in their path. We must not be ignorant of what could bring trouble and despair to our souls. This is what the Lord says in Jeremiah 6:

Stand at the crossroads and look; ask for the ancient paths, ask where the good way is and walk in it, and you will find rest for your souls. But you said, "We will not walk in it." I appointed watchmen over you and said, "Listen to the sound of the trumpet!" But you said, "We will not listen." Therefore hear, O nations; observe, O witnesses, what will happen to them. Hear, O earth: I am bringing disaster on this people, the fruit of their schemes, because they have not listened to my words and have rejected my law. What do I care about incense from Sheba or sweet calamus from a distant land? Your burnt offerings are not acceptable; your sacrifices do not please me.

This "disaster" or the "fruit of their schemes" (sometimes translated as "fruit of their thoughts", indicating it was premeditated and deliberate) was brought on by God's people who "have not listened to my (God's) words" and ultimately their disobedience. God does not accept the sweet smells of the burnt offerings in this case. Let us not do the same. While the aroma is still sweet, let us stop and smell the roses. Love is wooing us for all eternity and we should not turn our noses up at it.

The Inspiration of Honesty

If you ask my husband the reason he married me, he would tell you it was because of my honesty. He knew there are many liars who told many lies in this world. He decided to stick around to see if he could catch me in one. Thankfully that didn't happen. Truth is important to me personally and even more so spiritually. I saw no point in lying to my husband. Therefore, my husband never left!

When presenting the question "What does goodness mean to you?" to our eldest son Troy, his answer was "one hundred percent honesty." Having done my research on goodness, I knew that our guide alluded to this character trait.

After spending twelve months in Saudi Arabia with his wife, Troy experienced profound darkness within the construction site he managed. It was difficult, he said, to see how many of the ex-patriots, predominantly Asians, were treated. Their worth seemed diminished and irrelevant. Because they were treated this way frequently, they often worked with this same ethic. Troy told me that he would explain their tasks to them honestly and completely. He gave them the training that would improve their values and principles. There was no hidden agenda–just legitimate hard work that produced "good" results, including advancement of the project, improved morale, and loyal and self-respecting employees.

Loving our eldest son as his Dad and I both do has built a good connection with him. The importance that Troy places on honesty and openness in relationships has not come without cost in his life. Embracing affliction for good is no easy feat. However, it does produce peace and even prosperity into our souls. Take note of this scripture.

Before I was afflicted I went astray, but now I obey your word. Psalm 119:67

God uses the difficulties and suffering in our life to bring us to a door of opportunity. He entices us out of the place of distress to bring us into a place of prosperity and a place of no constraint. Through discomfort, he allures us. He entices us out of our distractions into the wilderness (a place of pure devotion) in order to give us our vineyards. In the "valley of trouble" is where the very "door of hope" opens up to us (Hosea 2:14-15). It is at our darkest hour when everything is about to change—for the **good**—unless we grow weary and give up. God does not want us to give up, but to endure.

Troy devotes himself to a life that continues to produce in

him honorable character. That character influences everyone he meets for their good.

You may ask, "What is an honorable character"? I would just like to touch on this in regards to goodness. The Greek word for honor, *doxa*, indicates reknown, glory, and splendor–especially a divine quality or an unspoken manifestation of God.

It is related to "honesty" as well, whose Greek word refers to someone being "good" and acceptable physically as well as morally. By definition, an honest person is marked by or displays integrity; they are upright, and not deceptive nor fraudulent. They are genuine, equitable, and fair. Honor, used in the sense of how one lives their life, means to be true to what is right or good.

To be honorable, however, goes further than simply being honest. By definition, an honorable person is to be venerated and greatly respected. It also is related to another Greek word which means valuable. Honorable people–people who keep promises–have integrity, and are true to their word. They are valuable and trustworthy in the eyes of others. In 1 Corinthians 7:23, it says that "God paid a high price for you". That word "price" can also be translated as "honor". Remember, you are a precious jewel in the eyes of God. Additionally, honor inspires reverence and awe, just as the Lord Himself does. This implies the outcome of an honorable character is holiness and righteousness, which should always be the goal in our lives.

Do you see the inspiration of the goodness of love in this definition of honesty and honor? Love's depth of wisdom and insight deals sincerely with our heart. There is no ulterior motive. We have been commissioned and are in training to get the prize–eternity in the arms of our beloved!

*Finally, brethren, whatsoever things are true, whatsoever things are **honest**, whatsoever things are just, whatsoever things are pure, whatsoever things are lovely, whatsoever things are of **good** report; if there be any virtue, and if there be any praise, think on these things! Philippians 4:8*

Righteousness and purity were two other words given to

me by individuals describing goodness when I asked my question. One friend described her husband as an example of what goodness meant to her. Imagine that in today's world! Another young man expressed goodness as living with morals and ethics based on virtue. I think love is well-pleased with this kind of fruit.

The Fruit of Goodness

The book of Galatians records goodness as a fruit of the spirit and Ephesians elaborates:

For the fruit of the light consists in all goodness, righteousness and truth and find out what pleases the Lord. Ephesians 5:9

Our soul is complete when it is fitted with goodness. Our nature becomes useful in love's hands bestowing honor when the fruit is fully matured. We become fertile soil, eager to learn and ready to bear fruit.

But the seed on the good ground are they, which in an honest and good heart, having heard the word, keep it, and bring forth fruit with patience. (Luke 8:15)

Here's still more from the Song of Songs, where Solomon describes the sights, sounds, and smells of what goodness and love do when they fill our senses:

Flowers appear on the earth; the season of singing has come, the cooing of doves is heard in our land. The fig tree forms its early fruit; the blossoming vines spread their fragrance. Arise, come, my darling; my beautiful one, come with me. Song of Songs 2:12-13

Chapter Fourteen
Peace

How can two walk together unless they agree? Amos 3:3

The bride will never forget the sequence of events that occurred that final weekend of their mission trip in that remote Middle Eastern village. At least once a week, the groom called together his closest friends to have dinner with him. They would celebrate the week's successes, talk strategy, and joke around with each other. On this trip, Lily and the bride were always present at these get-togethers.

Although many travelled with him on these trips, over the past few years, he had settled on a small group of friends whom he had shared his most intimate times, including meals, drinking, and deep conversation. He talked often of his ideas on how to help improve people's lives and also how to approach the next day's events and the coming weeks. He talked a lot about his father, for whom he obviously had great love, admiration, and respect. It wasn't much different on this Thursday night, although the mood was more somber than usual.

His team of workers lived very modestly, basically having left all of their possessions behind to join the groom on his excursions around the world. After all, they were living among people who essentially had nothing, so it wouldn't have seemed right to do otherwise. They had set up a few tents on the outskirts of the village where everyone stayed. They slept on the floor in sleeping bags. Each tent had a simple low wooden table, so low it didn't require chairs. They sat on the ground at the table for meals and also to prepare their food and supplies to be given to the people during the week.

Outside, they built a wood fire in a stone pit near the main tent to cook meat, beans, bread, and other hot foods in various cooking pots they had. Inside, they sat around the table to prepare fruits and vegetables, as well as bundle medicine, soap, toiletries, paper goods, and other supplies that they distributed to the people who came to them.

As needed, they taught the local people basic health and survival skills, as well as gardening, food preparation, and ways to improve their lives. In turn, they also learned from the more industrious people whose families had lived there for generations, some of whom had more advanced skills in surviving in this area themselves.

And always, the groom would speak to his small group of friends during their meals together, telling them his ideas about life, love, compassion, respect, and dignity. They ate together, told jokes, and enjoyed each other's company. They also shared their own personal struggles, including their fears, their hurts, and their opinions on various subjects. They even fought and argued with each other–anyone would who lived in such close proximity for extended periods of time, especially in these conditions.

Anyone, that is, except for the groom. Sometimes to the chagrin of even his closest friends, he always said and did the right thing. It sometimes drove the others crazy how he was so consistent in his behavior and never seemed to have a bad day–at least he never showed it. His own friends and even people he would help would get angry with him and say mean and hurtful things to him–but they knew he didn't deserve it and he never returned the favor. He would always remain calm, and was very slow to anger. In fact, he would go out of his way to show compassion and understanding to those who treated him badly. His ability to forgive was extraordinary.

There was that time on a previous trip when they had just had several successful days of helping hundreds of people who came to see him and his team, assisting them and sharing his message with them. He had been on a roll that week, and many people came to hear what he had to say. There was much healing going on, both physically and emotionally. It was one of the best trips they had had up to that point. But, then some of the locals saw that they could take advantage of the situation, and turned the main tent they were using into a way for them to make a quick buck, selling inferior or even broken battery-powered products to the people, basically ripping them off, and then refusing refunds. The groom found out and was livid. He basically kicked those men out of the tent, and asked them to not return until they were ready to treat what was being done there with respect. That was the one time his friends saw him get truly angry. They agreed that was the best way to handle that situation.

On this Thursday evening, they gathered for dinner in one of the smaller tents in the usual way. But, the feeling of this dinner was different. The groom seemed disturbed about something, almost distraught, and he was talking in unusual terms, even for him–relating things that were apparently about to happen. He kept talking about himself as if he was going to leave them, but they didn't understand what he was saying. Then, he dropped a real bombshell on them.

"One of you is a traitor who has been plotting against me. He is in this room right now, waiting for the right time to turn me in."

The group was dumbfounded. He was always warning them to look out for charlatans and people who could fool them, even those who made so-called humanitarian trips or did the kind of missionary work and unexplained things that his group did, but for the wrong reasons. He told them to look out for people who wanted power, acclaim, money, or other personal gain–and did not do charitable work simply because it was the right thing to do. But, never had he accused any of them of being one of those people, or even saying that one definitely was going to turn him into the authorities or get him in trouble in some way.

They also knew that the government didn't always agree with what they were doing wherever they went, and they had heard that this particular area was especially belligerent to outsiders, especially those claiming to offer help to their citizens. Most of the time, governments tolerated them because they did do good things for their people, even though the trade off was the control they lost–for example, losing the ability to ration food and supplies to keep them at bay.

After hearing the groom's claim, his friends immediately balked at what he said. Everyone denied that they would ever do such a thing. They continued their meal in silence, but the groom had more to say.

He began distributing the Khubz bread, a type of flatbread or pita common to this area. The pitas were so large, they had to break them apart and share them. He raised his bread in the air. As he did this, he spoke.

"Take this bread and eat it. It's being broken for you, just like my body will be."

They looked at each other, confused. Was he making a joke? They usually could tell when he was joking around, and this wasn't one of those times. He seemed dead serious.

Then, he raised his glass of beer, one of the only luxuries that they indulged in at their dinners. It was a reddish lager brewed locally and sold by several merchants in the city. Although it is thought by many to have originated in the Middle East, beer had become increasingly hard to find, and even made illegal in some countries. In the area they were, it was legal, and they could find beer and other alcoholic beverages fairly easily. A few of the guys always purchased some alcohol in a nearby town, and the groom was fine with that, even enjoyed drinking with them, as long as they didn't overdo it. They usually went to town for a few bags of ice along with other supplies every day and put the beers in a plastic cooler that kept them cold. They would drink it on special occasions to celebrate some of their successes.

"Drink up, guys! You've done some good work these past few weeks, but my time is coming to an end. This is like my blood that you are all drinking. With it, I hope that the world can share in a great victory and come to understand that what I am about to do is for everyone."

Eating his body like bread? Drinking his blood? Did the groom have a cannibal fetish? Was he preparing them for the coming zombie apocalypse? Did he have a fascination with vampires or something? What did he mean when he said "what I am about to do"? What was he talking about? They didn't get it, and the expressions on their faces showed that. It certainly didn't make any sense to the bride who was sitting with him. She glanced over at Lily. Her friend just sat there, smiling, but the smile had a certain knowing sadness in it too. It was a strange scene.

When they were done with dinner, a couple of the guys got their guitars out and they sang a few songs as a group. The groom always enjoyed live music and sang along with them. It changed the entire mood and helped them deal with some of the heavy things the groom laid on them, but they still knew something was up, but unsure what exactly. They decided to take a walk as a group outside in the early evening, along the mountainside where olive trees grew. They began talking amongst themselves. The groom knew they were worried for him. But, what he had to say next didn't help.

"I know you all are concerned, but I am just telling you what I know to be true. Tonight, I will go away from you and you all will leave me as if you didn't know me."

One of the group, whose nickname was Rocky, spoke up.

"Even if all the others leave you, I never will. I'm with you for the long haul."

"Even you, Rocky, will pretend you never knew me," the groom answered him. "Before the morning, you will lie three times to the authorities and deny being my friend."

"What?!" exclaimed Rocky. "How could you say that?"

"Because it's the truth," the groom said.

"Even if I have to die with you, I would never do that," Rocky protested.

The others agreed with Rocky, and said they would stay with the groom even if something happened to him.

They were starting to come back down the mountain, and several of them were ready to call it a night.

"Hey, where's Ike?" said one of them. The group looked

around and noticed he wasn't with them. Isaac added quite a personality to the group. He was smart, serious, and a good negotiator. He was also a bit of a loner, so they weren't too surprised when one of them recalled he had said he wanted to stay behind to run into town for some supplies they would need in the morning.

At that, several of the group began heading back to their tents. But, the groom wanted to stay out a little longer. He liked going to a particular garden of one of the villagers that had a sitting area. He asked Rocky and a couple others of their group, brothers Jimmy and Johnny, to go with him. He often liked going to this garden to relax his mind, focus his thoughts, and meditate deeply on the day's events. He told them it often helped him prepare for the coming weeks and provided him inspiration for what he would tell the people that would come to see him and hear him speak. Rocky, Jimmy, and Johnny were very tired, but they agreed to go with the groom as he requested. When they got there, the groom asked them to stay behind at the sitting area.

"Could you stay here and watch for anyone who may be coming by?"

"Who would come by here this late at night?" Rocky asked him.

"Please...just keep watch for me," said the groom.

At that, he left them and walked a little further into the garden alone. They watched as he walked ahead about 30 feet along the garden path. He then knelt down and began talking to himself–loud enough for them to hear him. They heard him address his father, as if his dad was right there with him. They could hear the anguish and pain in his voice. He was pleading with his father to prevent what was about to happen to him from happening. They didn't understand what he was talking about. They heard the groom say that he wanted to do what his father would have him do, which was typical of him to say.

The groom's three friends were so tired, they slumped over where they were sitting and fell asleep waiting for him. After a few minutes, the groom returned to them. Finding his friends asleep, he was disappointed with them.

The Absence of Love

"Guys! You couldn't stay awake for even a few minutes and do what I asked? Please stay awake a little longer and stand watch for me."

All three men expressed their apologies and promised to stay awake. The groom went back into the garden and resumed his meditating and talking out loud. After a few more minutes, his friends fell asleep again. The groom came back to them, and was upset that they had fallen asleep a second time. Again he went back to the place where he had been kneeling. And again they fell asleep. This time, he woke them up, saying:

"Wake up! It is time for me to be taken away from you. My betrayer is here!"

At that moment, they heard noises coming from outside the garden, and some loud voices and mumbling. The men turned toward the sound. They saw several armed military personnel and police from the city coming toward them. There were even some people dressed in civilian clothes, some carrying knives and baseball bats, that Rocky recognized from some of their meetings the past few weeks in their main tent.

Then, they all saw Isaac, who was with the military and the police, seemingly in charge of the mob, leading them over to where the four friends were standing. He walked directly up to the groom, and reached out to hug him.

"Greetings!" Ike said, as he gave him a hug and kissed his cheek, which was the custom in the Middle East for a friendly greeting between men.

"Friend," said the groom. "Do what you came for."

A military official stepped forward, grabbed the groom's arms, put them behind his back, and slapped handcuffs on him.

"You are hereby under arrest," he said. "You are being charged with crimes against the state, including being a spy, usurping governmental control, inciting riots, and going against the established morality and ethics of our society. You are to appear before your accusers tonight."

At that, one of the others in the crowd, apparently a friend of the groom, reached out with a hunting knife and slashed at the head of one of the military guards, cutting off his ear. Blood was everywhere. A fight ensued, but was quickly contained by the other officials there and by the groom himself, who spoke.

"Put away your weapons. Those that live by violence die the same way. If I wanted, I could put a stop to this whole situation. But, I am not going to. It was meant to be. It must happen this way."

The military group then hauled the groom away in handcuffs. Rocky, Jimmy, Johnny, and others who were on his side fled the scene.

~

When the decision to love someone is made, whether that is with God or man, a union is formed. In most cases, this is bound by a contract. Whether with God or man, both are spiritual commitments; however, only one, the one with man, is considered in this world to be the law of the land. In either case, the question is posed: "How can two walk together unless they agree?"

What are we agreeing on? Let us look at the spiritual commitment in the book of Romans.

*Those who live according to the sinful nature have their minds set on what that nature desires; but those who live in accordance with the Spirit have their minds set on what the Spirit desires. The mind of sinful man is death, but the mind controlled by the Spirit is life and **peace**; the sinful mind is hostile to God. It does not submit to God's law, nor can it do so. Those controlled by the sinful nature cannot please God. Romans 8:5-8*

You and I are not supposed to be controlled by our sinful nature. If we are, there is no pleasing God. In fact, it is "hostile to God" and does not give us the ability to submit to and follow God's law, including the spiritual commitments to God and, in legal marriage, to our spouse. If we allow the Spirit to control us, we have "life and peace." Let's focus on peace for a moment.

What words or descriptions come to mind when you think of "peace"? Quiet surroundings, a vacation getaway perhaps, easy-going and carefree living? A brook, stream, or flowing river with only a gentle breeze blowing. An open field in the country, with deer, rabbits, and some cheerful birds singing their songs to each other. How about lying in a hammock out in a meadow or maybe stretched out on a lounge chair on a secluded beach, the waves lapping up on the sand, with your favorite drink in hand and maybe some soft music playing somewhere?

Peace is a concept, but to some it's also a feeling, a state of being, and a place. A place where there's no fighting, no arguing, no problems at all. The opposite of war. Peace and love–they go together like peanut butter and jelly, salt and pepper, or apple pie and ice cream.

No pressure, no worries, no hate–not a care in the world. It's the best parts of what living and "life" seems like it should be, but isn't always. Is that your idea of "peace"?

In the Greek, the word peace is *eirene*, which is the equivalent of the Hebrew word *shalom*. It's the most common greeting given fellow Jews, especially at the time of Jesus, similar to our "hello". But, more than just a simple "hi", it was the wish of both parties to offer and hope for "peace" for each other. "Peace be with you" was a common greeting Jesus gave to his disciples. This peace is the desire for tranquility in the soul, not affected by outward circumstances or pressures. The original word implies completeness or wholeness. Those with true peace are whole, complete, orderly, stable, and not wanting of anything else to make them happy and contented. It is not necessarily the absence of conflict, but instead it is the presence of God no matter what conflict is going on.

That peace that comes to our heart from our commitment to God and His Spirit is a foundational peace in our relationships as well. It provides us the backbone, the strength, the willpower to reject Satan and fight against our sinful nature. In fact, this spiritual commitment is considered a prerequisite prior to commitment between a man and a woman in marriage. I did not know this prior to my decision to marry my husband Michael. Don't misunderstand me–I did know the difference between right and wrong. But, I didn't have the clarity I have today about the battle taking place for my soul spiritually. I don't think most do.

In order to have "peace", we must be able to overcome the obstacles in life. Looking solely at man in this world, it doesn't appear we are forming alliances of peace that are sustainable. Did you ever wonder why? Why is it so difficult for people to get along in this world? Nations seem to be in an uproar. Terrorist attacks and military strikes are carried out daily somewhere in the world, and are a constant threat to America and this generation. The worldwide economic downturn has plunged many into despair. Suicide is at an alarming rate. But, where are we spiritually?

Falling Away

Spiritually, many are falling away. Post-modernism and the idea that anyone can believe in anything is also giving rise to a rampant apathy in many individuals and even in families. If anything can be believed and all faiths have equal footing and argument, why believe in anything at all? This apathetic approach to spirituality has given rise in many countries, including England and more recently in the United States, to a militant opposite belief that seems to be sweeping the country: atheism.

Unlike traditional atheists, the neo-atheist variety is their equivalent of hardcore Christian evangelicalism. This group promotes their ideas and recruits members through various organizations, especially vocal on websites and Facebook pages devoted to "proving" God doesn't exist through their militant belief in Darwinism and their ridicule of Christianity. They are especially vocal about the "rights of unbelievers" when it comes to public prayer or Christian holiday celebrations. The professed denial of anything supernatural has been embraced by an increasing number of people in their twenties and thirties. Many of these people were raised in the church, or at least by parents who professed some kind of Christian belief, but some of those parents have even fallen away themselves. Many have suffered through divorce or the loss of a parent, lack close friends, have isolated or closed themselves off from family members, or have given up in trying to assign a bigger meaning to life. Many also suffer from drug or alcohol abuse, which are at their highest rates ever worldwide. They struggle with their own identity and self-worth, both personally and professionally, so have thrown up their hands in despair. Many are actually successful financially, and pursue and indulge in life's pleasures without caring much about the ultimate consequences of their actions, accountable to no one but themselves. The idea of no eternal hope, no life beyond our earthly existence, is a logical one to these people.

Of course, Christians are not free from many of these struggles and temptations themselves. For example, divorce is as common inside the Church as it is outside. I am not proud to admit that I am in that number! The difference is that Christians are accountable to a loving God who does provide that hope and reason for living, those "plans to give you a hope and a future" as God promises to Jeremiah. I believe one of the most important things we can do to resolve the turmoil in our individual lives or as a nation is to reason with God.

Study to Show Thyself Approved

It has been my great pleasure to travel considerably in this world speaking to various people, including Hindu, Muslim, Jew, and Christian. I have heard many stories, and people have varying degrees of how they express their faith. I have a Japanese acquaintance who put it this way to me: "I am a Buddhist, but not a very good Buddhist". Why? What was she and others like her telling me?

When posing a question to my Indian friend in the Middle East, I discovered that his belief system had been formed out of his life experiences. I think that may be so of many of the so-called "religious" people in the world. Let it be known here and now, that I do not consider myself a "religious" person, though I am fully aware that many people in this world would. In the sense that it is a general word applying to faith or worship (such as "pious", "devout", or "godly"), I strive to be "religious". But, I believe our guide defines the term "religious" in the sense of being hypocritical or overly righteous, demonstrating religion as if putting on a show for others, rather than living out your faith for the glory of God alone. In Matthew, Jesus warns against this.

Beware of practicing your righteousness before other people in order to be seen by them, for then you will have no reward from your Father who is in heaven. Matthew 6:1

Regardless of any "religious" upbringing, I have to be careful not simply to use life experiences as my teacher, as that could get me in trouble. We must be earnest in the reading and study of scripture as our guide. Otherwise, we won't know what is expected.

Personally, I know that I was born and baptized into the Methodist church system. After spending the majority of my life going to church, and even going through the system, I was basically unaware of Methodism. The Book of Discipline, published by the United Methodist church denomination even today, and updated and amended every few years, is filled with what this denomination believes. I'm sure there are some very good things in it, some which I probably would agree with and even practice in my own life today. However, it is a "religious" book which is not required reading when we have the Bible. I did not read it as a youngster, and do not intend to now. So, judging from my own life, I guess I could join my Japanese acquaintance by saying, "I am not a very good "Methodist"!

So if I don't consider myself "religious", then what? I'm not sure there is a single word for it. I'm even hesitant to call myself a Christian because of its connotation in today's world, but that's what I am–a follower of Christ. The denominations are filled with people who have not read the discipline of their religion but, more importantly, have read very little from the Bible, our very guide we have been discussing.

Time Magazine ran an article on Christians many years ago asking questions in a survey format, one of which I recall was, "Do you read the Bible"? The majority responded "No." The truth is we cannot become a Christian just because our mother and father declared us so. Still, we are considered in the United States of America the largest Christian nation in the world. Why does it surprise us, then, to find in the United States an ever-widening gap between what fellow so-called "Christian" denominations and believers actually believe?

I am in love with Jesus Christ and the Spirit of truth that He promised He would send us. As a student of the Bible for the last thirty years of my life, I can now firmly state that I, like Paul, boast only that I live so that Christ might live in me. There is the line of demarcation in me: I am in fellowship with the heavenly Father because I believe what He said about His son. It wasn't my plan, nor would it have been my idea. Remember, however, that my ideas failed me before I was twenty-five years old. I made a decision to ask Jesus into my heart. When He came in, I was no longer just a warm body on a pew in a church building, or for that matter a "Christian" not going to church. God accepted me the way I was, but had no intentions of leaving me that way. For the first time in my life, I had the first glimpse into what peace meant, that foundational peace that every believer of Jesus Christ acquires when they give themselves to Him. I had begun my journey anew in this world, and this time I was going to read the guide.

The Enemy Revisited

Until and unless we make this decision to follow God and to read the Bible, the owner's manual for our lives, we are in a war with ourselves that we cannot win. The denomination or religion doesn't matter, as long as the one true God is in our lives–only then can we overcome and have peace. But, that doesn't mean we don't have conflict. Understand that we are still at war!

Our enemy has been clearly made known both in this book and within our guide. The enemy has a name: Satan. Peace will not be accomplished in our souls until our enemy is defeated in us. As it says in Ephesians 6:11, we are to "put on the whole armor of God" so that we "may be able to stand against the wiles (devious or cunning strategies) of the devil." This includes "your feet fitted with the readiness that comes from the gospel of peace" (Eph 6:15) and "the sword of the spirit, which is the word of God" (Eph 6:18). This "sword" represents our guide. Can you hear the battle? Can you feel it? What part of your day has been lost or stolen that seems irretrievable? Has it been weeks or months or even years since you have felt that peace in your soul? Let me tell you, as one who has been brought back from defeat, love does know the way. You can overcome. You can find peace.

*And the **peace** of God, which passeth all understanding, shall keep your hearts and minds through Christ Jesus. Philippians 4:7*

There is a great deal more to be said about peace than I choose to detail in this chapter. My goal is to secure the path of peace that love has for us, and realize, as with all fruit, that it begins with a "seed of its kind". Seed develops in good ground. It takes time and must be nurtured for maturity to bring forth the fruit of peace.

Seek God

How maturity is attained with love, joy, peace, patience, kindness, goodness, meekness, faithfulness and temperance planted in our lives is important. These fruits of the spirit cultivated in us will last for all eternity. You *can* take it with you!

When a Christian passes on from this world to the next, all of the fruits of the spirit will be experienced to their maximum potential. When we show an example of this fruit now, we are bringing that little bit of heaven to earth with us. When we love each other despite our problems, when we are patient and kind, even to those that our human nature says don't deserve it, we are experiencing just a taste of what the glorious afterlife will be like, when the groom is united with her precious bride.

We need to develop these fruits, such as peace, to have the harmony in our souls for the nations of the world to have the opportunity for their own peace. Without it, none of us are safe. Let's therefore seek after peace, as much as it is possible on our part to do so that by definition we may manage a state of national tranquility.

The terms of peace have always been substantial. Even according to our guide, we must give up "everything". However, "everything" refers more to a condition of the heart than it does to material things. Many wealthy men in the Bible were considered godly and righteous men, including great kings like Abraham, Jacob, David, and Solomon, the latter who "passed all the kings of the earth in riches and wisdom" (2 Chronicles 9:22). In the New Testament, Joseph of Arimathaea was a "rich man" and a "disciple of Jesus" to whom Pontius Pilate delivered the body of Jesus.

Material possessions may simply check the incentive of our heart. Most live in this world as if their accomplishments and worldly possessions define them. They don't! And they didn't for those wealthy men of the Bible. They used their great wealth and power as a means to an end. That end was to seek God and attain that true, eternal peace that only comes when one's heart is in line with His. So, how can you prepare your own heart and seek God in that same way, to achieve that same kind of peace?

For he (Jesus) himself is our peace, who has made the two one and has destroyed the barrier, the dividing wall of hostility, by abolishing in his flesh the law with its commandments and regulations. His purpose was to create in himself one new man out of the two, thus making peace. Ephesians 2:14-15

In this verse, the "two" being referenced are the Jews and Gentiles (non-Jewish people). However, Paul makes the point that, regardless of your differences (whether in belief, age, wealth, stature, or any other things that separate us), you can now be united through faith in Jesus Christ. In His body, a body that was broken for everyone, He reconciled the differing religious views and groups in the world by his suffering on the cross and subsequent resurrection. Through Him, everyone can put aside their differences as we all have access to the same Father by one Spirit

(Eph. 2:18).

There is a way for peace to rule and reign in our souls in this world. How bad do we want it? It will not be accomplished with our own terms and conditions, but in each person's sharing in that new creation, that "new man", that lasting peace. Are you willing?

Chapter Fifteen
The Gifts

Repent and be baptized, and you will receive the gift of the Holy Spirit. Acts 2:38

The bride was deep in thought about that series of events in the Middle East when she was interrupted by her best friend again. Rather than a disturbance or disruption, being interrupted by Lily was, most of the time, like being hit with an unexpected cool breeze on a hot summer day. Lily swung around the corner close to the back row of seats where the people were gathering to watch the ceremony, and laid this interesting question on the bride.

"You know how much you are loved?" Lily said with her usual sweet tone.

"How much?" the bride asked, jolted out of her memory.

"Well, take a look at the gift table around the corner," she said.

The bride stole a quick peek around the right corner at the long, white-clothed, table against the wall. It was filled with all kinds of beautifully wrapped boxes with bows, fancy gift bags with colorful tissue paper sticking out, and enveloped cards in an assortment of colors: red, purple, pink, green, yellow, and blue. Just about all the colors of the rainbow were represented. She was amazed. Where had all of these gifts come from? Surely she was undeserving of all of this appreciation. Then, she realized many of the gifts must be there because of the groom, and she felt guilty.

"Overwhelming, isn't it?" Lily said, before the bride could say anything. "Well, don't forget that I had something to do with it too."

"I..I won't" the bride managed, feebly, not fully understanding what Lily meant.

"Enjoy your walk down the aisle. Wait for the cue. You will know when it is time. I am so proud of you! I love you."

"Thanks," the bride said. "I love you too."

With that, Lily left her. The bride glanced up, and, in the distance, she saw the groom waiting for her at the front of the room. She pulled her head back quickly, making sure she avoided his eyes. She didn't want to break from tradition and have her groom see any part of her in her wedding dress before the appropriate time. With that one glance, she was immediately thrown back in her mind to his arrest by the authorities in that small village in the Middle East.

When the events of the arrest in the garden were related by Jimmy and Johnny to the others at the groom's camp, everyone was shocked and dismayed. The bride was devastated. How could this happen, she thought? Out of fear, several of the group simply ran away to hide. They found out that Rocky had decided to follow the groom and the military officials into town, but at a distance to avoid being brought in as well.

Some of the groom's camp were angered and planned to attend the public accusation, most likely to take place in the open courtyard downtown. Others agreed to attend, but everyone thought it best to not travel in a group, and instead split up individually to avoid suspicion and not be arrested in a similar fashion. Regardless, most were scared for themselves and the fate of the groom. They were convinced he had done nothing wrong, and would be released tonight once the police chief of the city would be able to discuss it with the other officials. Surely, the groom, who normally handled himself in a public forum with great aplomb and fortitude, would see to it that nothing would happen to him. He would talk his way out of it, they all agreed.

The bride sought counsel from Lily, who seemed unusually distant from the situation, but also seemed to know something that the bride and everyone else didn't. When the bride questioned her on it, Lily only offered that what was happening was just "meant to be" and that we would all simply have to endure what was about to take place.

"What does that mean?" the bride implored Lily, trying to get more information.

"I can't say anymore," Lily responded, "other than to tell you that you need to trust that everything will work out the way it was intended."

This did not help the bride understand the situation. She simply had to take Lily's advice, as her best friend wasn't giving out any more information. The bride took a back road to the downtown area. When she got there, the situation looked grim. There was a large mob of people outside, and she overheard many of them mention the name of the groom, and were talking about him as if he were already a convicted criminal. She couldn't believe the accusations they were making against him.

Finally, she saw Rocky, who was distraught. Rocky took her aside privately, behind a row of hedges just outside the courtyard. He related to her that the officials and the leaders in the village and the city were trying to pin false charges on the groom. It appeared they wanted to execute him.

"Execute him!" the bride said, in utter shock. "For what?!"

"They have very strict laws here about behavior outside the norm of their culture and society. Punishment is severe for what you and I would consider minor offenses."

"Well, what can we do?" the bride asked.

"There's nothing we can do but wait it out. They may not have any more information for us until the morning."

At that, they decided to separate. The bride hid in some nearby bushes, a short distance from the courtyard. She stayed awake most of the night, but at some point must have fallen asleep.

In the morning, the bride was awakened by shouts from the crowd. She walked out to the courtyard a ways to get a closer view. Three people were standing up on the second floor landing of a government building on the north side of the courtyard. The man in the middle was the police chief of the city. To his left was an accused murderer that they had been holding for a few weeks. The bride recognized him from news reports earlier in the month. To the police chief's right was the groom, who was wearing only a simple pair of shorts and a ripped-up, blood-stained T-shirt. He had several cuts and bruises on his arms, legs, and face, as if he had been beaten, cut with a knife, or lashed with a whip. The bride heard the police chief yell to the crowd.

"But, what crime has he committed?"

"Kill him!" several shouted out.

"Why! What has he done?" the police chief shouted back.

"Kill him!" several others shouted.

"Give him to us and we'll take care of it," another shouted.

It took a minute to understand what they were talking about. It was the time of the spring festival in the city, and it was a tradition at this time to let one prisoner go free. The crowd had just opted for the accused murderer to be released in the traditional good gesture by the police chief. Apparently, the fate of the groom was left to the people.

The bride was in utter disbelief. How could this be happening? She was mortified, sick to her stomach, and began weeping bitterly. She didn't want to draw attention to herself, though, so she suffered in silence, standing behind several others in the crowd who were yelling and wanting to take part.

"You have your wish. I will release this man to your custody. Do what you need to do with him." He pointed to the groom, and made a gesture to have him taken away.

After several minutes, the groom reappeared on the ground floor in the courtyard in handcuffs. Several men were standing around him. One held a video camera. Another had a burlap sack. A couple others had clubs-one was of the billy variety, the kind a policeman would use. The other resembled a baseball bat, the Louisville slugger type. The groom turned to look out to the crowd. One of the club-wielding men hit the groom hard in the rib cage, and he bent over in pain. At seeing this, the bride cried out and winced. She folded her arms on her forehead and fell to her

The Absence of Love

knees in the dirt. She began sobbing, unable to think. Then, she heard more shouting, and looked up again.

Near the groom, another man emerged. He was holding a huge sword, so big that the others stood clear of him. It had two handles on one end and a blade about three feet long and about four inches thick at its widest point. The men began shouting, some of them chanting. The man with the sword began shouting as well, motioning with his hands for the group to proceed. The ones with the clubs struck the groom several times on his back, sides, and shoulders. Others pushed him to get him walking. The groom suddenly fell, moaning in pain. They pulled and dragged him to his feet again, hitting him at the same time. He was finally able to move forward again.

They appeared to be walking in the direction of a hill that started about a hundred yards west of the courtyard. A larger crowd began to gather, as more people heard the shouting, and even began to join in. Apparently, the group in charge wanted everyone there to be able to witness this event, and would capture it on film, probably to post a video on the internet or share it with international news sources. They wanted to make sure everyone knew what they were doing. They taunted him, spat in his face, humiliated him. They continued beating and throwing punches at the groom as he walked, making sure he suffered excruciating pain on the way to the place of his execution.

The bride couldn't bear to watch the one she loved suffer such atrocity. She stayed behind and at a distance, unable to think coherently and unsure what to do. She watched as the groom passed by her, with the bloodthirsty crowd chanting, shouting, even laughing at him. She felt helpless and alone at that moment. She couldn't imagine what the groom was feeling.

~

Where love exists, gifts seem to be involved. In every romance, courting, and relationship, love likes to express itself through giving. Gifts are exchanges in the proposal with the engagement ring, anniversaries, and other celebrations. Of course, there are the wedding gifts themselves, showered on the bride in separate get-togethers and on the happy couple on their wedding day. And, for any time at all, gifts are, for many, that ultimate expression of love, both in the giving and the receiving of them.

But, we aren't talking about simple, physical, natural gifts here. We are talking about the supernatural variety. In our story of love revealed, the conduit–the channel in which these supernatural gifts pass to us, like flowing water rushing through a pipe or electricity passing through hot wires enclosed in a protective tube–is clarified in our opening scripture.

Repent and be baptized, and you will receive the gift of the Holy Spirit. Acts 2:38.

This becomes the first supernatural gift–that of the Holy Spirit. The absence of love, in which the gift is ultimately rejected and the pursuit of the things of this world becomes man's aim, provides a counterfeit of the real thing.

In Acts 7:39, Luke the apostle references the time Moses led God's people out of Egypt. He indicates that the gift of the land that God had promised for His people was discarded by them. "Our ancestors refused to obey Moses, and instead rejected him and in their hearts turned back to Egypt".

Ultimately, the freedom from bondage that the Israelites had, a gift from God, was refused by them–maybe not physically, but in their minds and "in their hearts", the ultimate rejection. The Jews entry into the land of Canaan was finally left to Joshua to complete, who led the children and grandchildren of the original group into that land "flowing with milk and honey". This abundant land is compared in the Song of Solomon to the beautiful bride herself: "Your lips distil nectar, my bride; honey and milk are under your tongue." What an image!

However, even in Joshua's time, there were problems when they finally got the land promised to them. While the Canaanite kings had been destroyed by Joshua, it remained for the individual Israelite tribes, such as Judah and Simeon, to battle and conquer the remaining Canaanites from the land. In the book of Judges (chapters 1 and 2), we are provided an explanation for the downfall of the nation, as well as the reason why God left them. He had warned the Jewish people before, and reminds them of that warning when they are in the land of Canaan, continuing to battle the idolatrous people there:

At that time I also warned you, 'If you disobey, I will not drive out the Canaanites before you. They will ensnare you and their gods will lure you away'. Judges 2:3

And disobey they did:

The Israelites did evil before the Lord by worshiping the Baals. They abandoned the Lord God of their ancestors who brought them out of the land of Egypt. They followed other gods—the gods of the nations who lived around them. They worshiped them and made the Lord angry. They abandoned the Lord and worshiped Baal and the Ashtars. Judges 2:11-13

The Israelites did the very thing God had warned them about so often. At first, they simply tolerated the Canaanites, but soon the Israelites were imitating them. The nation that was to be special and set apart from the evil ways of the Canaanites now embraced the very sins that had brought God's anger upon them.

Clearly, there are parallels to our world today. Mankind, in our covenant with God, was supposed to be special, holy, and blessed. However, there are conditions to this promise: we must accept and live up to the terms of the agreement. His love for us is unconditional, but that doesn't mean we are blameless and have no accountability ourselves.

So, the "Giver" of this gift of freedom, it seems, had to leave before the individual could receive it, and so it was. Moses had to leave the scene, to make way for Joshua to provide God's gift of the land of Canaan to the Israelites. And, God Himself left the Israelites, even in the land of Canaan, for a time.

Finally, God in human form, Jesus Christ, had to leave in

order to return as the ultimate gift for mankind. God loves us so much that when we make the decision to have Jesus Christ as our Lord, we are "born again" and granted ultimate "freedom", and receive the nature of God as a gift. This nature is both "holy" and "spirit". What gift could be greater than the very nature of God Himself?

But, who would receive this gift? It would be given to those who would "believe, repent and be baptized" (Acts 2:38) How it would be given varies. Let's focus on the gifts themselves.

The Gift of the Holy Spirit

There is a similarity between an engagement and subsequent marriage of two people to what is experienced when receiving the Holy Spirit. Just as two people decide to live as one under the same roof, so it is we accept the gift of the Holy Spirit into our lives. A ring is generally an outward demonstration of an inward decision when two lives join to live as one. The agreement is essential to the receiving of the engagement and wedding rings, and so it is with the gift of the Holy Spirit. Essentially, we give permission for this Holy Spirit to unite with us. We announce that our heart's desire is to live in fellowship with Love.

But who really is the Holy Spirit? In our guide, the Holy Spirit is a person. He is always referred to as "He", not as "It". I don't think, however, that the "He" refers to the Holy Spirit as a "man" or "male" in any human sense. The "He" is more out of language custom or convenient pronoun representation to the Personhood of the Holy Spirit, similar to the Father reference as the Personhood of God the Father. The point is that "He" is someone, not something.

What qualities or characteristics does the Holy Spirit have? Well, for one, He speaks (1 Timothy 4:1). He also teaches us (1 Cor. 2:13). He knows the thoughts of God (1 Cor. 2:11). He prays for us (Romans 8:26). In the book of Isaiah, He is called the spirit of wisdom, counsel, might, understanding, knowledge, and several others. He is the Comforter, Counselor, Helper, and Advocate

(John 14:16), the Power of the Highest (Luke 1:35), and the Breath of the Almighty (Job 33:4). He even has emotions–it is possible to grieve him (Eph. 4:30). The Holy Spirit, then, is more than a mere force or power, as in "May the Force be with You" in Star Wars lore. He is more than simply inspiration, enthusiasm, or excitement, although he can inspire us, and also enthuse and excite us nonetheless. He is also more than psychological terms such as our conscience or our subconscious, although He can affect both of those things, even in our dreams. He is the very Spirit of God. In fact, He IS God!

From our guide, the uniting of the Holy Spirit with us is expressed through one's decision to "believe, repent, and be baptized". All of these decisions and actions may take different forms. "To believe" is the overall decision to agree to the love covenant. "To repent" is the acknowledgement that we are truly sorry for the mistakes we have made, the sins we have committed, and to realize that it is God alone who has the power to forgive us and enable us to live eternally with Him. "To be baptized" is the public declaration and affirmation of these decisions to believe and repent. In our guide, John the Baptist tells his converts "I baptize you with water. But one more powerful than I will come. He will baptize you with the Holy Spirit" (Luke 1:33; John 1:33). Of course, he is referring to Jesus Christ.

The bottom line is that the two who enter into the love covenant have come to a crossroad and, instead of deciding to depart from one another, decide to carry on life's road together. Engagement culminates in marriage. So it is with the Holy Spirit.

Let's not get ahead of our story, though. Love expresses itself vocally when two people announce their engagement to one another and to their family and friends after that. Their hearts are excited about what the future will hold for them, including children, home, and the joining of two families. The first gift, an engagement ring, symbolizes the union. However, life isn't perfect after that. The saying "Life is not a bed of roses" is actually not true. It is just like having to care for that "bed of roses". A wedding is like buying the seeds for a rose and staring at the beautiful photo of the roses on the package. We think we know what it can be like.

We imagine the joy and happiness a love relationship can bring. We hope for it. We long for it.

However, marriage is the process of caring for that rose plant. All roses are beautiful to look at when they are grown, and the idea of having a "bed of roses" in a full rose garden that you can call your own is enchanting and exciting. But anyone who has grown roses knows that they are difficult to care for. They come with many thorns to hurt us. They need constant sun, good soil, lots of water, and nurturing. The foundation needs to be strong. Although the promise is made, that doesn't mean, at least in the life of a married couple in this world, that trouble won't come. Temptation from the enemy is a constant struggle, and we will continue to sin and have to ask for forgiveness of our spouse in the natural world and our spiritual "spouse" in the supernatural.

In our guide, the Holy Spirit is also referred to as a seal of the union that takes place at the time of our acceptance of this gift from God. God, who is Love, "sets His seal of ownership on us, and puts his Spirit in our hearts as a deposit, guaranteeing what is to come" (II Corinthians 1:22). Ultimately, that is the wedding feast!

The Gifts of the Spirit

Our guide also describes several "gifts" that the Holy Spirit Himself bestows on those who believe and come to accept that first "gift" of the Holy Spirit Himself. The Holy Spirit's gifts are many, but come from the same Spirit of love. I don't know how God selects individuals to receive His gifts. He said only that they are dispersed as He chooses. Knowing your spiritual gifts will help you find your way and place in God's kingdom and in an individual church as you speak and minister to others.

*Now to each one the manifestation of the Spirit is given for the common good. To one there is given through the Spirit a message of **wisdom**, to another a message of **knowledge** by means of the same Spirit, to another **faith** by the same Spirit, to another gifts of* *healing by that one Spirit, to another **miraculous powers**, to another **prophecy**, to another **distinguishing between spirits**, to another **speaking in different kinds of tongues**, and to still another the **interpretation of tongues**. All these are the work of one and the same Spirit, and he distributes them to each one, just as he determines. 1 Corinthians 12:7-11*

This passage from I Corinthians does not hold the exhaustive list of spiritual gifts. (See also Romans 12, I Peter 10-11, and Ephesians 4:11) There are many gifts and some people have more than one. One gift is not superior to another. All gifts come from the Holy Spirit. They are a manifestation of God's love. This book will not go into these "gifts" in detail, nor the reasoning why I believe these gifts are alive and well and freely given out today. That is for another book.

The point is that a relationship involving two people who spend time together develops and matures. The purpose in the relationship with the Holy Spirit in our lives is to accomplish the same thing. We can eagerly desire these spiritual gifts. We may even experience these gifts ourselves, but there may be times where our discernment fails us. Still, it is "love" itself, expressed by Paul in Corinthians 12:31, that is the "most excellent way". Although we should eagerly desire these spiritual gifts, we are to follow the way of love–to love God with our whole heart, soul, and mind and to love all people. Otherwise, we become that "noisy gong or clanging cymbal" that we have mentioned earlier. Even if other things do fail us, love never fails.

It appears we are given different gifts according to the grace given us. Grace is that unmerited love, the one we didn't earn. This is important because it is the gauge that keeps us from thinking too highly of ourselves while, at the same time, honoring and serving one another with it. Administering this grace requires the designation of love given in the beginning of our story. Namely, God is Love!

There is a great deal more to know about the gifts that are given by the Holy Spirit and many books have been devoted to doing such. It is not my desire to do so here. What does seem relevant to me is to clearly focus on God's gift to us.

Gifts are Not Earned

God's love for us is genuine. Being in love with God is our choice. Every one doesn't decide to do so. The seed I would now like to sow does not require an affirmative to this choice.

The gifts of the Spirit are given because the Giver chooses to do so. That's not so different from how it is for you and me. I can choose to remember my parent or a friend in a special way on a special day when I decide to. The difference is that these gifts of the Spirit you and I cannot give.

For it is He who gives them to each one, just as He determines. I Cor. 12:11b

We can do nothing to earn the gifts of the Spirit. The teaching on this subject incorporates "Do not think of yourself more highly than you ought" (Romans 12:3). If I receive a gift, such as a two-carat diamond ring, then I may just feel very special. We can be assured that, though we are loved and special, the gifts of the Spirit are not what declare that to us. We are defined by the love itself. That is why it is so critical to understand as much as possible about love while at the same time trying to generate growth. Any development apart from love must be re-evaluated.

His Gift, His Son

For God so loved the world that He gave His only begotten Son that whosoever believed in Him would not perish but have everlasting life. John 3:16

Again we return to this verse, the foundation of Christianity. Not only does John author the incomprehensible heart of God towards us, but further testimony is given of God's declaration in regards to the gift of His Son. Listen!

And this is the testimony: God has given eternal life, and this life is in his Son. He who has the Son has life; he who does not have the Son of God does not have life. I John 5:11

Eternal life is wrapped up in the person of Jesus Christ. If we "have Him" ("believe in Him"), we can partake in this life, a life beyond the grave. Just as He defeated death and sin, so we have the ability, through Him, to experience the eternal bliss of heaven when we die.

Redefining Love

Men and women who have committed their lives to one another in marriage often separate. Why? What happened to their love? What happened to their commitment, their promise, their "until death do us part" declaration?

I've long wanted to redefine "love" because my own desires of it profited me the counterfeit variety more often than not while looking for it in my life. God can and does work all things together for good for those who believe in Him, so the false love that appeared to me at every turn now accomplishes glory to Him. In experiencing so many times the false love, God allowed me to move that much closer to what true love is. He taught me, and in time I learned. Eventually, the one true God and one true Love was known to me.

Love chose to create me, to give me physical life on Earth. Love also chose to be in a relationship with me, to fellowship with me, even if I did not acknowledge its existence. Love exposed itself to me when my efforts to discover it on my own proved fruitless. In the midst of my despair, I was painfully aware that I had exhausted my own ability to create love in my life. In my world, I experienced an absence of love by allowing myself to be exposed to the Great Imposter. Satan is not patient. He will not wait for you. He works continuously on anyone who is willing to be tempted. Fortunately, God *is* patient–and he waited for me!

How love was revealed to me has been written about in this story. It is a true story–and it is true in more ways than one. It is a story about my life and love's revelation to me. It can also be a true story for your life. It is the story of Love's plan to be restored to "whosoever would believe" in Jesus Christ.

What we believe in many places around the world is formed by what our family and traditions have developed. We are human and to err is, as well. My family, by many standards, was good to me and I pray that this is so of my readers as well. Regardless, it is just a type and shadow of the real thing. For the individual who selected to bring this book home with them, you know that something in your life remains to be sorted. On the day in my twenties when I declared, "If there is anything left of me, God, that You can do anything with, You can have me," my life changed. Everything I have written about has come out of my exhaustive desire to find love. Once Love revealed itself to me, there was an acknowledgement in my soul. My response today remains consumed by it.

Lest any reader think that, because of my dedication to love, I am perfect, let me reveal further my surprise in this regard. My sinful nature can appear at any time. There is a need to daily desire love to expose my heart. Recognizing that a person's heart is deceitful was a hard pill for me to swallow. Apart from God/Love, I can do nothing. Believing in His plan for love is essential.

In this world, we will have trouble, but fear not for He has overcome all. We will continue to have trouble in our lives because there is often a huge absence of love on any given day, in individuals, families, and communities. Knowing the promises love has made to us helps us to hold the course. When pain and suffering linger, we can cling to faith and that gift from God of the Holy Spirit and His Son, Jesus Christ, which will produce hope and a harvest of righteousness.

Chapter Sixteen
The Wedding Feast

As a bridegroom rejoices over a bride, so your God rejoices over you. Isaiah 62:5

The bride was jolted out of her waking nightmare by the sound of music. The wedding march finally began. It was her cue! It was time for her to start her long walk to the front. She was flustered. She felt her face getting beet red. She also began to feel queasy. She was nervous and scared. What was she going to do?

She couldn't believe the time was finally here. She had to compose herself. But, there was no one with her at that moment. She felt like she was on her own for the first time in a long while. She took a deep breath. She heard the music beckoning her. She heard Lily's voice say "It is time." She didn't see where the voice was coming from, but it still comforted her. She took another deep breath, and then stepped out from behind the wall.

She was now standing in the middle of the threshold of the door in all her glory. She didn't feel glorious, though. Her wedding dress with all of its adornments was beautiful, but she didn't know it at that moment. She held a bouquet of flowers in front of her, tightly in her hands. She looked down the long, red carpeted center aisle leading to the front of the room. The walk looked miles long. Breaking from tradition, there was no father of the bride to walk with her either. Her parents had passed away long ago, and there was no one on this planet to take their place. She would take this walk alone.

She took her first step. She looked up slowly. She glanced around at all the people. Everyone was turned around toward her. All eyes in the room were immediately upon her. She felt loved and respected by many, but condemned, ridiculed, and violated by others. She felt her muscles stiffening, and her stomach began tying up in knots. She was nauseous, but she tried to will that feeling away. She knew she had to keep moving forward. She began to move her legs and feet very slowly, taking each step carefully and methodically, so that she wouldn't trip on her dress. She also wanted to drag out the seconds as they passed by. She didn't want to rush the walk since she decided long ago she didn't want to forget any of it, no matter how it turned out. For so long, she couldn't wait for this moment to arrive. Now that it had, however, she wasn't sure what to make of it.

After a few steps, she looked up and saw the groom ahead, in his wedding tuxedo. He was dashing, breathtaking, magnificent. Everyone and everything else in the room seemed to fade away from her view. Standing there, he was the most beautiful sight she had ever seen. As his face started to come into focus, their eyes locked onto each other. Everything changed at that moment. The tightening in her stomach and her nausea immediately subsided. She felt totally free and fully alive. She realized why she was here, why she was doing this, and what her true life's purpose was. She continued her slow walk, and it was unreal to her, almost like she was in a dream. She was used to being the focus of attention, as she had had quite a bit of that attention in the past, but not always in a good way. The blissful experience of her bridal walk now was beyond words. What joy she had at that moment! She was actually to be united with her groom, the one who meant everything to her. It was a joy matched only one other time. As she walked down that aisle, staring at the groom's face, she was whisked away to the memory those several years ago when the unexplainable happened–after the nightmare of his torture and death.

The bride watched the crowd take the bloodied groom

The Absence of Love

away. She felt paralyzed, numb, and unable to move or think. After several minutes, she finally had the strength to move. She dragged herself back to where she had stayed most of the night, and slumped down in utter despair and hopelessness. She didn't know what to do, and had no one to turn to. At that moment, she realized how exhausted she was. She closed her eyes. She didn't think that she would even fall asleep. If she did, she hoped it would be forever.

Hours later, she was awakened, this time by a gentle nudge on her shoulder. Someone was whispering her name.

"Please wake up," the voice said.

The bride opened her eyes. It took her a second to realize where she was and what had taken place the night before and the first part of the morning. Her eyes were out of focus.

"It's time to wake up," the voice said, a little louder this time.

She realized she was staring into the face of Lily. The bride woke up with a sudden start, trying to sit up.

"Easy now," said Lily. "You've had a rough night."

"Rough...yeah...ohhhh..." said the bride, and she realized she was in pain from sleeping on the hard ground most of the day. "I must go to him. Where is he?"

"They have placed his body in a locked coffin inside a mausoleum with two armed guards outside. It's not safe to go there yet."

"He's dead?" said the bride. She couldn't believe it.

Lily did not answer her. Instead, she said "Come with me. It will be safer this way. I have a place we can stay with the others."

Lily helped the bride to her feet. They walked together and talked. Lily tried to comfort her with encouraging words, but nothing mattered at that moment except her groom was dead. After a time, they arrived at a building that she had never seen before, which had a back alley entrance. Through a locked door were two flights of stairs leading to a third story room that seemed like a good place to hide. When they opened the door, several of the groom's team were there. From the looks on their faces, they all seemed to be as miserable, confused, and distraught as she was. They also were frightened and on edge.

They spent the weekend there. Several of the men, including Rocky, Jimmy, and Johnny, had brought enough food and water to enable the group of them to stay there for several days. On the third day, there was a knock at the door. It was two of the women who had left earlier in the day to go into town. They were actually sent to go to the mausoleum, as Lily had instructed them to. They were so excited, they couldn't contain themselves.

"Listen! He is alive!" said the first woman.

"We have seen him!" said the second woman.

The two women looked at each other, nodding in agreement.

The group in the third-story room thought the two women were delirious. They weren't making any sense. Several of the groom's group, including these two women, actually saw him dead, his mutilated body discarded by the angry mob like so much trash. One of them, Joe, had even asked the police chief if he could help prepare the body and lay him for burial. With what the sword had done to him, there was no question that he was dead. Several witnessed the actual execution, and several more confirmed the groom's identity afterward.

"We all saw him dead. *You* saw him dead!" said one of the group.

"I know!" said the second woman. "But, listen to us! We went there, and he wasn't there. Instead, there was a man there dressed in a white suit who must have been from out-of-town. He was simply sitting in the mausoleum near the entrance, as if he was waiting for us. He told us he wasn't there–that he was no longer dead. He had come back to life!"

"Why did you believe him?" said one of the men. "Someone must have taken the body."

"Well, that's what we thought at first. But, then we *saw* him!"

"You saw him – what, alive?"

"Yes," said the first woman. "The man told us we would find him in the city. So, we went there. We went into a café on a side street for lunch. It was pretty empty–not much business. And, there he was sitting at a booth by the window. We couldn't believe it!"

Several in the group gasped. All were astonished. No one had anything to say for a few seconds.

"Did...did he look okay?" said one of the men, finally.

"Yeah, he looked fine. It was as if he hadn't gone through the whole ordeal. Apart from marks on his neck, wrists, and feet, his bruises and injuries all seemed to have healed. He was wearing chachi shorts, a casual shirt, and sandals–the normal clothes he always wore. He was eating a fish sandwich and drinking some beer."

The group was dumbfounded. They didn't know what to say. They started to wail, some of them whooped cries of joy, some cheered and yelled out.

"What? Ahhh...that's....that's unbelievable! Is he...is he coming to see us?" cried Rocky.

"No...he...he told us to tell all of you to come see him in the city."

"Where in the city?" asked Jimmy.

"Well, he didn't say where," said the second woman. "I guess he just assumed you'd find him."

They were all so excited they were not sure what to do first.

"Well, let's pack up and go to the city!" exclaimed Johnny.

The bride was amazed and astounded at the story of the women, as was the whole group. They honestly didn't know for sure what to make of it. Were these women for real? Could they have seen someone who just looked like the groom? If this was a hoax, it was a pretty elaborate one. The bride didn't think anyone in this group had the ability to pull something like that off anyway.

They all agreed it best to not travel together again. The military and city officials would probably be out looking for them still.

The bride was one of the first ones to go to the city. Once she arrived, it only took her a few minutes to find the groom. He was on a side street, visiting with a couple of the poor people in the city, doing what he always did–showing them kindness and compassion. She stood out of view of him, some distance away, his back to her. But, she could tell it was him, even without seeing his face. She watched as he gave them both hugs, and they turned and walked away from him. He then turned toward her, began walking, looked up, and then saw her. He stopped. She froze. Their eyes locked on each other. She had a hard time believing her senses at first. Was this really him in the flesh? She felt her legs running to him. It felt like a force beyond herself that compelled her to him. He put his arms out. She practically jumped into them, giving him a hug and a passionate kiss on the lips. It was the longest kiss they had ever had up to that point in their relationship. She just couldn't get over that he was alive!

"I told you I would return," were the groom's first words.

"I....I didn't know what you meant," the bride said.

"I'm glad you do now," he said.

"I'm so happy! I can't believe it's you," she said.

"It is me." was his simple reply.

They embraced again for several seconds, without saying anything. He wept, and she wailed loudly, then quickly muffled her cries against his chest and shoulder. He gently lifted her head so he could look into her eyes. Then, he said the strangest thing.

"I'm really hungry," the groom said. "Could we go get something to eat?"

The bride smiled at him, almost laughed, and nodded.

"I love you," the bride said.

"And I love you. Always have, always will," the groom replied.

~

I don't know if I've ever really understood the scripture that opens this chapter. How can a God–One who is all-knowing, all-powerful, all-present, and who knows the most intimate details of everyone on this planet–rejoice over me like a "groom rejoices over his bride". I mean, how am I that special to a Being like that? A human groom has one person to focus on–his human bride. I have seen many a groom in love with their bride, at least on their wedding day. I believe I have experienced that more than once, at least in the beginning. But, a God who is responsible for billions of people? How can that God be so focused on me–little ol' me. The human mind can't fathom it. I do admit that, at this point in my Christian life, my loving God does occupy my thoughts the majority of my time–at least, He is never far away from the front of my mind. On the other hand, remembering that He "rejoices" over me in the focused way that a newlywed couple fawns over each other…well, I don't think I really do get it.

This is a revelation to me–a recognition that I spend a lot of my effort trying to love God. After all these years, it still doesn't always come easy. Some days, it is a struggle. After all, bringing every thought into obedience with the mind of Jesus Christ is a full time occupation, isn't it?

I can understand how difficult it must be for you to broaden your concept of what a "loving God" really means. This concept is still difficult for me. Most things in this world do not last very long, so the idea of eternity–such as an eternal life or eternal love–must seem incomprehensible to most people. Still my motivation beyond the writing of this book–my heart's desire–is to know the kind of love that not only created me with a purpose, but rejoices over me like a groom over his bride! I want that in my life. I need this kind of love enduring in me, both in this life and when I pass from this world and go into the next. And, I want that for you. I hope that you do too.

Maybe those sharing this journey with me will have to dream a bit to consider themselves loveable, but it is the truth based upon our guide–God's word. We were loved for an eternity even before we were placed in our mother's womb. Think about that for a moment. If God is all-knowing, and has always existed (since he wasn't created, he being the Creator), he always knew the moment I would exist as a human being. I try to think about what God must have felt the moment before I existed, the moment that egg and sperm united to form me. Did I get last-minute instructions, maybe somewhere in my DNA, about my purpose in that moment? Did He tell me He loved me as I was sent on my way into this world? Did He say to me, "Don't forget me?"

Though I have spent the better part of my life looking for love, I often forget God loves me. For the atheist, this may indicate that there is no God. For me, it simply indicates that I don't meet with His standards. I have made the choice to accept God's covenant in my life. In Jeremiah 3:14, he declares that "I am your husband". My declaration is to believe that He is.

Anticipation

There are books, magazines, reality TV shows, and websites devoted exclusively and extensively to the preparations a young bride and groom make before their wedding day. Most of these preparations cost money to achieve–lots of money. The efforts of individuals joined together to carry out these desires are exhaustive. Almost more than the ceremony itself are the plans made for the reception, not least of which is the food. For any bride and groom who plan to have even an average size wedding, especially in America, the meal, including set up of the tables and seating for the guests, the catering, the wedding cake, and all of the trimmings can be an enormous and expensive task. The feast at the reception with all of the guests celebrating the bride and groom's union is the highlight of many weddings. It is a joyous occasion.

So too, the preparation work in me involves years of work to be united to my spiritual groom. It is true for most people. For those who make that decision to say "Yes", many years of development must follow–in fact, a lifetime is needed. We are constantly maturing as human beings, continuing to develop those "fruits of the spirit" all our lives. Those who have Jesus Christ as our example will never be satisfied, or should never be satisfied, with where we are. We must strive to be that perfect bride, that perfect groom. We will never be "perfect", but should always look for ways to improve. Our guide commands that we do. Nevertheless, we will always be loved, and that decision to commit guarantees that we will be united with our spiritual spouse for all eternity. So, why do I sometimes question the preparation work necessary for faith to accomplish this in me?

Did I take too big of a leap from a wedding in the natural world to one that takes place as the door closes on time into eternity? I hope not, because the essence of this love story culminates at just such a banqueting table. Listen!

Hallelujah! For our Lord God Almighty reigns. Let us rejoice and be glad and give him glory! For the wedding of the Lamb has come, and his bride has made herself ready. Fine linen, bright and clean, was given her to wear. Revelation 19:6-8

The wedding of the "Lamb" represents the sacrificed and resurrected Jesus Christ who has come to take His bride, which symbolizes both the Church as a whole, as well as each individual believer. If our preparations have been done right, the "bride" will have "fine linen" to wear that is "bright and clean". Again, we have a symbol from our guide of clothing representing who we are as people. This fine, bright, clean clothing represents the righteous living or good deeds of God's "holy people". Such people are sometimes referred to in our guide as the "saints". We should all desire to wear such "fine linen"!

Our preparation for this wedding feast is extensive. Love has invested a great deal in you and me–in time and cost. In fact, it will cost us everything we have–most of all, our hearts. He wants us to love Him. We need to remember how he rejoices over us.

Love Revealed

Earlier in this story, we discussed the cost that God paid for us–His life! God sacrificed his own son, Jesus Christ, on our behalf. In doing so, He gave us the gift of life and the gift of love. No sacrifice before or hereafter will ever be greater. Our acknowledgement of this (or denial of this) does not make it more or less so. Love accomplished for us the will of God, and we can decide to confirm or deny the authenticity of it. The choice is ours, but the work to establish a way for love to come into our hearts was already completed long ago. In John 19:30, just before he died on the cross, Jesus said these words: "It is finished." Indeed.

The absence of love in our lives indicates a crossroad we each come to at some point. The choice we all have allows us to recognize our need for love to be revealed in us. Our parents can't do this for us anymore than we can do so for our children. It is the most important decision we ever make. The question you must ask yourself is this: Do you believe in love?

If the answer is "yes", then redefining what that means is what the rest of our lives is all about. We will find out through all the senses–sight, taste, touch, hearing, and smell. These are the gates into our soul that transmit love.

There is a counterfeit to love that abuses those same five senses. The good news is that there is no point in our lives that we cannot recover love. Remember the contingency plan in the love covenant? Even when we fail, love does not!

There's more to reveal about love's plan and the "wedding feast". No matter how long you've been dreaming about your wedding plans, Love has held you in His heart longer. Let's eavesdrop on what is recorded through the spirit of prophecy given to John for just such an occasion.

I saw the Holy City, the new Jerusalem, coming down out of heaven from God, prepared as a bride beautifully dressed for her husband. And I heard a loud voice from the throne saying, "Now the dwelling of God is with men, and he will live with them. They will be his people and God himself will be with them and be their God. He will wipe every tear from their eyes. There will be no more death or mourning or crying or pain, for the old order of things has passed away. Rev. 21:2-4

Now that's some plan. Imagine–no more crying, no more pain, no more sadness, and especially, no more death. For eternity!

Where we are to live eternally has been on the heart of Love a very long time. Details are given to this dwelling place. Read all of Revelation 21 for more. No home will be more glorious or more at peace than the one Love has spent all of eternity developing.

I don't know if I was a fast learner, but looking throughout history, I know that everyone did not make the choice that Love challenged us to make. May you, dear reader, be encouraged–time still exists. If you have not already, receive in your heart today the great gift of love–eternal life with God. It's His plan and His way. There is no other. He will accomplish what He began in you–a good work, and the hope of glory!

He who was seated on the throne said, "I am making everything new!" Then he said, "Write this down, for these words are trustworthy and true." He said to me: "It is done. I am the Alpha and the Omega, the Beginning and the End. To him who is thirsty I will give to drink without cost from the spring of the water of life. He who overcomes will inherit all this, and I will be his God and he will be my son. Come! I will show you the bride, the wife of the Lamb. Rev: 21-5-9

"I am making everything new!" is a declaration, a prophecy, a promise. Love kept this promise to me. Though I continue my journey daily, overcoming the obstacles that keep love engaged in my heart, I have heard the voice of the Spirit. In my heart, Love touched me. As it says in Psalm 34:8, I "have tasted and seen that the Lord is good". Can you smell the banquet at the "wedding feast"? He has prepared it for you and me. "Come!" is an invitation to fully enjoy the riches of the banqueting table. And what a feast it will be!

Epilogue

Once she focused on the groom's face, the walk down the aisle was like the most amazing dream she'd ever had. She felt like she was floating in the air to him. Her mind and all of her senses told her this was a real event, but it was a different reality than she had ever experienced up to this point. A wave of pure joy began overtaking her. It was like she wasn't in control of her body at all. It was like it belonged to him.

The ceremony went by in a flash–the lifting of her veil, the exchange of vows, the rings, the pronouncement, and the kiss–oh, the kiss! It was long, deep, and passionate–a preview of things to come. Her heart could barely be contained. It leapt in her chest.

During the ceremony, a strange thing happened in terms of the guests who were there. The ones who were friends of the bride and groom all stayed to the end, and presumably would also share in the reception and wedding banquet immediately following. The others who were more the onlookers or ones who did not agree with the union that was taking place seemed to either leave before it was over or simply fade from view. It wasn't clear to the bride, since, when she looked up at the end to be announced for the first time as the newlywed couple, those people had all vanished. It's like they were never there to begin with.

After the ceremony, the groom took the hand of his bride as they walked to the reception hall, which was just a short walk from the ceremony room. The touch of his hand was electric. It was like he was super-charged with a magnetic field when she was close to him, and even more when they touched. It was almost unbearable just to hold his hand at first. But, then she settled in and got used to it, and it felt so good–like a peaceful warmth all over her body. It was like stepping into a super-heated hot tub, which seems too hot to the touch at first, but then your body slowly adjusts to its warmth and it feels so good, you don't want to get out. Except this feeling was a thousand times better than that.

They approached the reception hall, but then he stopped them a few feet short of the double doors, which were closed. He turned to her, still holding her hand.

"Are you ready?" the groom asked her, with anticipation in his voice.

"Yes," the bride said simply.

He let go of her hand briefly, gripped both double doors, and flung them open simultaneously. What a sight they were treated to! The reception room was an architectural wonder inside, with vaulted ceilings, marble pillars, wood arches and elegant trim throughout. There was an amazing array of lights, colors, sounds, and smells–the latter coming from the magnificent display of food on the banquet table. It was overwhelming. Gorgeous chandeliers, eye-catching criss-crossing draperies, elegant wood carvings and paintings on the walls, and the most beautiful music she had ever heard being performed by a multi-piece orchestral band–not quite jazz, not quite classical, and not quite rock n roll, but it had elements of all of those. Guitars, horns, piano, strings, and woodwinds, with a choir of vocalists. It was quite a unique sound, like nothing she had ever heard before. And those harmonies–amazing!

The banquet table was enormous, with the largest assortment of food she had ever seen: fancy hors d'oeuvres and cheeses; every color of vegetable and fruit you could think of; steak, chicken, fish, lamb, and beef dishes; an assortment of casseroles, rice dishes, pasta dishes, soups, and salads; all kinds of world and international dishes representing every country on Earth, it seemed; and many other exotic-looking but exquisite dishes she couldn't identify that appeared to be just as delicious and expertly prepared as everything else on the table. Even the garnishments and the decorations on the guest tables were amazing–candles, flowers, handmade crafts, and several other pretty accoutrements. It was by far the most amazing spread of edible delights and decorations she had ever seen. The bride, groom, and all of their invited guests ate to their heart's and stomach's content.

"From now on, you will be able to eat like this any day you want," the groom told her.

"Really?" said the bride.

"Really. And this is just the beginning of the wonderful life we will share together. Follow me."

The groom got up and helped the bride out of her chair. They walked hand-in-hand to the other side of the reception hall to what appeared to be an exit to the outside.

"Where are we going?" the bride asked.

"I will show you," the groom replied.

The groom pushed open the door leading to the outside. When the door opened and they stepped through, they were standing at the edge of a large open meadow at the base of a grassy hill. It was the lushest, greenest grass she had ever seen. She looked up and the sky was an unreal deep-blue color. At the top of the hill was a magnificent mansion, which appeared to be at least three stories tall and was enormous in size. She couldn't believe what she was seeing.

"Is that…" she gasped.

"Yes," he said. "That will be your new home now. Our home."

It was unbelievably beautiful from this distance. She couldn't imagine what it was like inside.

"I will carry you," the groom said. At that, he lifted her up and cradled her, wedding dress and all, into his arms. He began the walk up the hill toward the mansion.

To purchase a copy of this book,
search online for *The Absence of Love* by Sandra Lindsay.

To find out more about Spiritual Meat Ministries Incorporated,
visit the SMMI website at http://www.spiritualmeat.com